CW01551500

I Am Bigger Than Me

FRANCES PUNTER

Dedication

To remembering who we really are

Aknowledgments

To God, the source of all creation, as I am everything with you and meaningless without you

My angels, for always being with me

Mum and Dad, for everything

My family, for the love and memories we share

My children and grandchildren, you are my world and mean everything to me

Sis, for our special soul connection

My soul family, those already in my life and those yet to appear

Thank you everyone that came and went in my life, I grew because of you

I love and appreciate you all

X

Contents

Introduction

I would like to share some of my experiences with you. It's not an autobiography by any means as there are many experiences yet to be told and many still to be created, just a few chosen memories that I feel were significant in showing me who I really am.

As the saying goes, "Words don't teach, it's life experience that teaches", so I am bringing these experiences to you in the form of words, not so much to teach but to share some of the moments that taught me so much. In viewing myself in the mirror I hold up I believe, you too, may see aspects of yourself in the reflections.

The reflections at the end of each story are my thoughts, lessons and sometimes questions and are there to gain a deeper understanding of each experience, dissecting and squeezing every last drop of insight out of them for growth and expansion. In each experience were diamonds just waiting to be uncovered and sometimes I had to dig deep to find them.

As I look at my life, I clearly see the reality I live is of my own making. I didn't consciously choose some of my experiences but the vibration I was emitting did. As I change my thoughts and feelings, my life changes. I am in control of my reality and life is a mirror reflecting back to me what I am giving out. I also know I can change any aspect of myself that I have outgrown and become any aspects I prefer to be. We cannot always help what we see along our journey through this life as we live in a world full of others, all having their own experiences, but we are responsible for what we keep focusing on. In becoming the observer and having a healthy awareness of what Is going on around me I can see the problems, the things that don't serve humanity as a whole, the things that need changing but, by taking my attention away from them and focusing my energy on the solutions, I give power to the outcome I desire instead of feeding the issue.

Our thoughts have so much power and we are creating in every moment. Before anything is created it is first a thought. The chair you sit on was a thought before it was a thing; it was energy before it was matter. Therefore, our thoughts really matter.

We are beings of light wrapped in a physical form and the bigger and best part of us, our essence, is a conscious energy. When we go inwards, looking past the physical form, we see we are emitting signals out into the universe. We are the attractor of each experience, each and every thought sending signals to our body, which are picked up as either an uncomfortable or pleasant feeling in that moment. This then vibrates a frequency out from your heart centre, rippling out to be picked up by whatever matches that vibration. The beauty of it is, if you are not happy with what you are bringing into your life, you can take an inward glance and in consciously changing your thoughts to ones of a higher nature, it will lead to better feelings, and you then send out your new improved vibration.

With our free will we are able to put out into the world whatever we want to create, be it positive or negative to the whole but remember, you will then have to experience what you have created.

I have a deep desire to make the world a better place for all and I know it starts with me. I cannot change the world holding on to bitterness, revenge, fear and grief. I change the world by my Loving presence and my vibration.

By aligning myself, consciously connecting with source, the creator, the higher power and opening myself up to the flow of pure light energy that is always flowing to me, I can receive inspired ideas of a better way of being. As I gain control over my thoughts and emotions, I allow the vibrations of my heart to ripple out in the frequency of love so everyone I come into contact with will have gained positively in some way by our connection. In sorting out my thoughts about what and how to be happy, I know I am not on a journey to happiness, but a journey of happiness, and to be happy in whatever I am doing in each moment is the key to having a happy life and bringing about more. If at any time I don't feel the flow, it's not because it isn't there, it is because the thoughts I am thinking are out of tune with its love frequency and, as soon as I change my thoughts to those of a higher loving nature, the flow returns.

Our natural frequency is Love. We were born with the harmonics of it in our hearts and anything not of love is unnatural to our minds and bodies, bringing us discomfort and pain. Those in pain don't know what to do with it so they desperately try to get rid of it by giving it to someone else, but it doesn't make It go away, it just spreads it around. We have to learn to release the emotions of the past as they are only there to show us that if we do something that didn't make us feel good then we know not to do it anymore. There is, therefore, no need to hold onto the emotions of the lesson as they serve no purpose, other than to weigh us down. You wouldn't carry around all the shoes you've worn from your journey from child to adult because you've outgrown them, just like your emotions, so let them go.

We are all unique sparks of the divine and have our own perceptions about life, who we are and why we are here. We are all living life through the lens of our own eyes and our contribution to the world is invaluable. We were born with gifts and talents to share with the world and each of us carries the crystal seeds of greatness inside us. In seeing ourselves and our vast potential through the eyes of the great poet Rumi we become, not just a tiny drop in the ocean but, an ocean in a tiny drop. We 'real-eyes' we haven't even begun to scratch the surface of what we are truly capable of when we align ourselves with source.

I want you to know you do not have to be somebody in the eyes of others to have something to say to the world, as everybody is somebody. Don't hide your thoughts, your ideas, your dreams. Share them and make them come to life.

My fellow Warriors of Light, I hope you enjoy reading my experiences as much as I enjoyed creating and writing them.

In love and in light

Frances x

Rainbow

Here I was, halfway up a mountain in the Costa Rican rainforest; it felt so surreal, so completely different from the view I was used to seeing. At home in London the buildings were all squashed together, and the trees were fitted in between the concrete, allowing nature just a tiny space to live. It was such a contrast. Here I was surrounded by trees of all different shapes, sizes and colours, each one playing such a significant part in sustaining the life of this amazing forest. Here it was the opposite; it was the buildings that were fitted into the tiny spaces.

As I listened to the sounds coming from the Howler monkeys in the distance, I thought how surprisingly small they were for the amount of noise they made. With such big bellowing deep voices, I imagined them to be at least twice the size they actually were. There was something magical in watching the different species of birds fly past, the red macaws, toucans and hummingbirds, the sights and sounds of nature had never thrilled me as much as being here. The white noise made by the insects, each one individually sending out its unique signal, was constant and was not only a sound but a vibration I could feel. The signals were instinctive, each tiny insect born knowing what to do. They didn't have to be told, they just knew and together they merged, sending a unified version of sound out into the jungle. They reminded me of an orchestra, the insects all playing their parts, their emitted signals meeting and coming together in a wonderful collaboration of frequency and sound. Throughout my life nature had always played a massive part in my growth, how I viewed the world and everything in it. When we open our eyes and really watch it, its cycle of life, its systems, its healing, there is an abundance of knowledge it has to share with us, teaching us so much more about ourselves.

My mind travelled back to the day Tracie and I knew we were

coming to Costa Rica. Our friends Oliver and Stacey had bought a house in Costa and were thinking of setting up a retreat and asked us if we wanted to come over to be part of it. We thought it was a wonderful opportunity as it was something Tracie and I had spoken about many times before. It was agreed that we would go over in November. This gave us only a month to sort out the details; one of the main obstacles was the money for our travel. We had no money available for the flights, let alone our stay, but not letting a little thing like that stop us, we agreed, and arrangements were made. Tracie and I spoke about our upcoming trip and all the wonderful experiences we would have and were eagerly anticipating an amazing time. We knew the money would turn up, we didn't know how but knew in our hearts it would. It was more than hope, it was a deep, inner knowing. A few weeks passed and our friends were due to come over to England for a short stay and were going to help us with booking the flights and we still had no money.

In the meantime, life went on and we carried on with our projects. We had arranged to have a meeting with a lady who was interested in the projects we had organised in the community. The day of the meeting Tracie couldn't make it so, rather than put her off, I agreed to meet her by myself. The meeting went well, and she was really impressed with what we had done and afterwards we began speaking about other things. I mentioned the opportunity that had presented itself to us and we both laughed when I told her we didn't have the money yet. Then a strange thing happened, we began to get very personal and spoke about our children. I was going through a tough time with one of mine and I opened up to her, suddenly getting very emotional. She hugged me and told me about a similar situation she had with one of her children and we instantly connected on a deeper level and we sat for quite a while, confiding, comforting and laughing. Before she left, she told me she would like to offer us £1,000 pounds towards our trip. She really wanted to and didn't want us to miss out on this incredible opportunity. I cannot tell you how that felt, and I thanked her and the heavens above for the wonderful gift and couldn't wait to share the news with Tracie.

Oliver and Stacey arrived a few days later and we sat looking at flights. We only had five hundred each and they were known to be double that but, low and behold, there they were, flights at five hundred pounds. We quickly booked, and it was all arranged. We were going to Costa Rica. Stacey was quite surprised about the cost of the tickets and a few days later looked at the prices again and they had all increased to over a thousand pounds.

I thought how wonderful it was the way it all fell into place, the universe surprising and delighting us the way it did, and knew it was our expectation and focused attention on what we wanted to happen and now we were here, living what we had created.

I sat there looking around at the beautiful environment feeling extremely content and allowed my thoughts to wander whilst my eyes scanned the sea in the distance. I smiled as my eyes came across the whale I had excitedly spotted on our first day here, until a very amused Oliver explained it was a rock. The sun that had showered us in light was now being hidden behind a very dark grey raincloud and everything changed very quickly. The birds had instinctively disappeared with the sun and the white noise suddenly became drowned out with the onslaught of rain hitting the ground. We didn't need to move from our seats, we were completely safe from it under the shelter of the wooden canopy and so I stayed seated and observed. I watched the rain hitting the pool and as each drop connected with the water, it created millions of ripples which all intermingled with each other. I thought this is what we are all like in a crowd, all sending out our ripples and interconnecting. If we could learn to appreciate and value each other for what each of us brings we could also play together in harmony in a unified version of sound. It was inspiring, sitting there watching it fall, not a drop touching my skin but being deeply touched by it. The burst didn't last and before long the suns warmth burst through the darkness, its time was over, and the sun basked us in its light again. Just like that the birds appeared, their colours seeming even more vibrant and vivid and the symphony that had been drowned out burst into life, becoming audible once more.

A hummingbird appeared in front of me, its little wings beating so fast I couldn't see them. It just hovered there effortlessly in mid-air, searching deep inside the flowers, going from one to the other. Its colours were incredible, the blues turning to green and then to blue again in any slight movement of its body. I smiled inwardly as I remembered the hummingbird is there to remind us that the sweetest nectar is found within.

Rainbows appeared after the rain, water droplets left by the rain struck by sunlight in a certain way, rain and sun, the beautiful contrast. I thought how important they both were, if there was only sun everything would dry up, and if there was only rain everything would drown, but together they created the perfect balance and when elements of them both come together, they can create the most beautiful rainbow. It all seemed so connected and representing us and our lives. I thought about the rainbow we have inside each of us, each energy centre with its own colour and its own frequency corresponding and assigned to different parts of our bodies.

I was pulled away from my train of thought by the sound of Tracie's voice asking our friends if they had seen many rainbows whilst being here. I smiled as she must have been in on my thoughts, which was no surprise as we were often on the same train. I imagined them to be outstanding as, in Costa Rica, nature really was at her best. A brief discussion about rainbows took place and Oliver got up to get the net to clear the debris from the pool. Oliver had walked round to the other side of the house where the outdoor shower overlooked the lush green mountains and where, in the early morning, the clouds looked as though they were waking up after a night in the forest and gently escaping from the top of the trees. Oliver shouted for us to come and look! We all got up very quickly and, as we turned the corner, saw the most magnificent double rainbow, it was so big and the colours so vivid and bright. It was breath-taking and we all stood there in awe, transfixed on its beauty. It was incredible, truly outstanding. After absorbing it for a while, we started to make sounds, trying to convey in words how it made us feel. It is unclear who said it, when such beauty takes your breath away, sometimes the thoughts that come into your head leave your mouth without it being a conscious action, but either Tracie or I said, "I wonder what it would feel like to be at the end of it, to have all the different colours pouring into you and to completely bathe in its light."

The next day arrived, and Stacey and Leslie had planned to take us to another waterfall. Costa Rica was full of them, each one so unique and magnificent in their own way. I felt calm and peaceful as I looked out of the car window, daydreaming. I recalled the beauty of yesterday's rainbow; I had never seen one like that before. It had the ability to take my breath away just thinking about it. I daydreamed a lot, I always have, and I felt totally in tune with nature as I sat looking out absorbing my surroundings, watching the birds and the trees go past. Oh, the trees were so green and lush, the density and the sheer vastness of the forest excited me, and I imagined the entire life just one tree held, all the insects, birds, animals and organisms that lived or passed through it each day. I had learnt that trees share nutrition with each other through their roots and marvelled at the thought of how so much takes place beyond our view. It's for us to open ourselves up to see, in deeper ways, the wonderful world we live in completely and fully. I visualised the roots of the trees, how far down and across they went, entangling each other and holding each other in a sign of unity and strength.

We arrived at our destination through a dirt track up in the mountain and parked up. This waterfall was unlike the previous one we had been taken to by our friends. I recalled the previous one had been high up in the mountains above their home. We had tracked through dense jungle, no path, just jungle, nothing but the slight sound of running water in the far distance to guide us. It was a long, hot trek but, oh, so worth it. When we reached a small clearing, it was as though the jungle opened up to show us a piece of its paradise, clear running water, the rocks, the sounds and nothing but mountains all around us. It really was in the middle of nowhere and, if this was nowhere, nowhere was heavenly.

The waterfall we found ourselves at was more known and had a path leading down to the water's edge. I looked around as we reached the bottom and marvelled at how the waterfalls were all so different and all so beautiful, the colours, the smells, and the sounds, everything so bright and alive. I looked at the massive boulder stuck in the middle of the waterfall right at the top. It was unusual and looked as though someone had strategically placed it there to stop its flow, but the sheer desire and power of the water, too fast and too constant, had simply gone around it. Finding the gaps and not allowing the boulder to obstruct the natural flow, it used the obstruction to create an even bigger spectacle than it would have been without it. I recalled how I had used my biggest obstacles in life to create and bring out something bigger and better in me; it was all a matter of perspective and I appreciated both the boulder and the water for the insight.

There was nobody else around as we put our bags down on the rocks and, as Tracie and I stood there, a beautiful rainbow suddenly appeared by the edge of the waterfall. Tracie and I looked at each other, immediately knowing it had been created for us, we had asked for it, we had wanted to know what it felt like to bathe in its light, to feel the colours going through us and here it was, appearing just as we'd arrived. We hurriedly took off our clothes, just chucking them on the rocks. We couldn't wait to feel it but, before heading in, Stacey warned us there were most likely fish in there that bite, but we didn't care, we had been given a rainbow. The universe had put all the elements together, conspiring to bring it to us and we both knew in our hearts we were blessed. If there were fish that bit in there, they wouldn't be a match for how we were feeling right now.

As we waded in, being careful not to slip on the rocks underfoot, I received an impulse to try to get it caught on camera. I thought how great it would be to get a picture of us in it so I hurried back to get my phone. As I picked up my phone, I passed Stacey to give Leslie the phone, asking her to try to capture us. I remember vividly reaching the rainbow, the water was up to my chest and there was a constant rushing sound of the water as it powered through the gaps, hitting the water below with great force. I could feel the light, the colours running through me as it danced and played in recognition with my own, and I lifted my hands up in the air embracing it completely, receiving it fully and surrendering totally to its light. I could see Tracie opposite me, playing in it and taking it in. I could see her clearly one minute, then the next she was iridescent. We laughed and played together in the rainbow for ages until the time came when, sensing the same thing, we looked at each other, knowing it was time to leave.

As we began to head back to the edge, I looked back at the rainbow as if to say goodbye, to thank it for its presence and the beautiful experience it gave us that would remain in our hearts forever. I thanked its creator, feeling nothing but love and appreciation and, in that moment, I felt connected to everything and everyone. I looked around at my surroundings, the rainbow, the beauty, this place, nature; I was captivated, knowing it all came from the same divine energy and, as I looked back once more, the rainbow had gone. There were a few more people around as we reached where Stacey and Leslie were standing, and I thought how strange it was that nobody else had joined us. They had heard our laughter and seen us playing and, instead of joining in, chose to watch us in our joy. I excitedly asked Leslie is she'd managed to get some pictures but, better than that, she had caught it all on video.

We stayed for a while enjoying the water, making stone piles and sliding down the much smaller waterfall before heading out. Tracie and I watched the video in amazement as, at one point in the video, we became unrecognisable and were just two beings of pure light. As we sat in the back of the car, both running over in our minds what had just happened, we listened as Stacey and Leslie replayed what they had witnessed. Tracie and I kept looking at each other, smiling, but unable to speak about it, the feeling far too intense and powerful.

We couldn't water this feeling down by using words, so we did what we usually do when we felt like this, we communicated energetically from our bubbles of joy. We returned back to the house, still full up to bursting point of rainbow light energy and began to try to explain to Oliver what happened. We showed him the video; thank God we had the video. Oliver remarked that it was a good thing Leslie had taken the video as it wasn't one of Stacey's strong points, capturing and taking pictures. I had no idea at the time, but my inner guidance did, and had guided me past Stacey to Leslie who captured the whole experience perfectly and completely, giving us something tangible to share with others so they could see for themselves the absolutely astounding experience we co-created with our desire. We knew we had experienced a miracle. We had asked for it and received it the very next day. We must have been so open to receive, no boulders or obstacles in our way and, if there were any obstructions, we didn't let that stop us, we just flowed powerfully through the gaps.

Rainbow reflections

As I watched the rain hit the pool, causing ripples that intermingled with each other, I could see so clearly how the vibrations and the energy each person radiates out affects everyone and everything it meets. We are always affecting or infecting, in every moment. When we start to choose the vibrations we send out, becoming aware of the power in each moment, we begin creating consciously rather than being led by our unbridled emotions.

Asking is the foundation for receiving and we asked what it would feel like to bathe in the light of the rainbow, and we received it the very next day. Before we landed in Costa Rica, we had talked about the spiritual journey we were about to go on. We expected miracles and were wide open to receiving them, and they were given to us.

We had no money when we arranged to go but knew it would come, we envisioned being in the rainforest and felt how it would feel to be there. We spoke about it and what we would do when we were there, and we brought it into our reality. Our expectation and excited anticipation of what was to come created the circumstances to allow it to happen. We didn't allow 'what is' to determine what would be.

When we were told about the fish this could have put us off if our thoughts took us to a place of fear, but we weren't vibrating in the energy of fear. Our vibration was so high that we knew, if we stayed in the vibration of love, and there were fish in the water that bit, their little teeth would not be a match for our love.

My inner guidance knew that Leslie was the one to capture the essence of us in the rainbow. I was led past Stacey to give Leslie the phone and, at that time, had no idea that Leslie was the one to capture this rare footage of us playing in the rainbow, fully capturing the moments of a miracle.

On later reflection I wondered why nobody else had joined us in the rainbow. There were people watching in awe from the sides, but nobody joined us. Perhaps they were content in just enjoying the show, or maybe they were not a vibrational match at that time for the miracle.

When I focus my thoughts back to that experience, I can still feel the power, the light of the rainbow colours as they shone through me, playing and dancing with the colours and light already inside me. I can see Tracie and her iridescent colours. I feel its power and I am so thankful that I now know what it feels like to bathe in Rainbow light.

As I was reflecting on this experience my mind wandered back to a time when I was a child, where I had desired something with a friend and our desire was met. I will take you to that place with me. The name of the experience is 'Sure-footed as a goat'…

Sure-footed as a goat

We lived on the ground floor of a block of flats, nicknamed the 'banana' flats. The architect had carefully planned it so that it curved in the middle, making its curve hug the large expanse of grass, and we lived right in the centre of its curve. It was a perfect fit as our home was where all the children seemed to come, whether it was for a needed drink, to get a bike fixed or a plaster for a knee, it was the heart of the flats and it was as though we were divinely placed there.

Parents were able to see their children as they played, creating a safe environment for us all. On the large expanse of grass many games were created and played, and many hours of fun were had. It was a great place to grow up; I had the biggest garden to play in and I had lots of children to play with, but my favourite friend was Karen. We just clicked. Karen loved doing the same things as me and was always up for trying new, fun things.

One morning, after finishing breakfast, I asked to go out and headed out of the door to knock for Karen. As I took the first step out my feet were caught by the biggest gust of wind imaginable. It was so strong and powerful, it almost knocked me over, at the same time whipping me around and pushing me forward. I laughed at its movement and power and, although its force almost took away my breath, it also exhilarated and excited me.

Karen lived on the second floor in one of the smaller blocks beside mine and, as always, my route to her door consisted of climbing over the railings leading up the stairs and climbing all the way to her door along the small ledge on the other side of the stairwell. I had to hold on tight, putting one foot over the other as the ledge was small and tight, and it was a long drop down.

Karen's Mum didn't want her playing out in the wind and suggested

I come in and play; we could play with Karen's dolls, she said, but Karen and I just looked at each other, 'Boring!', we said telepathically. It took quite a lot of energy and persistence trying to get Karen's Mum to change her mind but, after a while, we managed to convince her, and we headed out. Karen had a cyst on her eyelid that wouldn't go down and it was a little swollen. She had been to the doctor's and was having it removed the following day. The doctor had told her she would have to keep a bandage on it for a week after the procedure and we laughed at the thought of her looking like a pirate. I told her she was lucky, and I wanted one as well.

As we came out of the block the wind, excited to see us, played with our hair, our clothes, threw leaves in our faces and moved us forwards and backwards at will and we shrieked in delight at its playfulness. I received a thought… "I've got a great idea!", I said. "Let's ask your Mum for a bed sheet," so we quickly ran back upstairs, taking the stairs properly this time, as we were in a hurry. I told Karen's Mum my idea, but she refused and said there was no way she was going to let Karen use her bed sheet. Furthermore, she said, we should be playing something less energetic because of Karen's eye. We knew we had to tread carefully as she may just change her mind and make Karen stay in, so we quickly left.

I knew my Mum would let me have two sheets if she had them, so we ran towards my house with the wind nearly taking our feet from under us. I explained my idea to my Mum, and she gave me two old sheets and some string. Mum also cut some holes in the corners for us with her dressmaking scissors and helped me tie a corner around each of Karen's ankles. I told Karen to hold the other corners in each hand and I did the same. We headed out onto the grass and into the wind and were blown clear off our feet, taken backwards by a gust of wind captured by our sheets. We laughed hysterically as we attempted to get up, only to be knocked down and blown around again. I wanted to take off using the sheet and the wind to elevate me; I think I managed about 6 inches off the ground before being thrown onto the grass. I could see my Mum looking through the kitchen window at us, smiling and shaking her head. We laughed so much and so hard our insides ached with the strain. We spent most of the day laughing and playing with our parachutes and the wind until finally, completely exhausted, we undid the strings and headed to Karen's house. It was nearest, and she needed to wee.

As we entered her block, I handed Karen the sheets to hold as I climbed over the railings and we chatted as I put one foot over the other, holding on tightly to the rail as I went. On the way up we laughed at our antics and discussed how high and far we went. Karen confessed she was scared about them removing her cyst and, for a few moments, I felt her fear of the unknown but reassured her that it would be fine, and I told her again how I wished I was getting a bandage for the week so we could both be the same, and she wished I was too. As we got past the small landing before her door Karen told me to stop going up the stairs like that; she said, "It's really dangerous and one day you might fall, and it's a long way down," but I told her, "Not to worry, I'm as sure-footed as a goat." Then nothing. I don't recall anything apart from a distant voice screaming, "Frances is dead, Frances is dead!", and then the loud knocking of a door. "Am I? I don't feel dead but what does dead feel like?" I thought. Karen's Mum came racing down the stairs telling me not to move. I didn't move. I didn't even know what happened, but I was lying at the bottom of the block, near the steps. Karen was hysterical; her Mum took hold of her and calmed her down before telling her to get my Mum and Dad while she watched over me, making sure I was ok. The colour had disappeared from Karen's Mum's face, and she was as white as a ghost and her hands were shaking. I could both feel and see her energy trying to connect with mine, but it was unable to penetrate me as I felt too peaceful and calm.

Mum and Dad soon appeared through the archway and, although they spoke words of reassurance and comfort, I could see their energy. There was only a low glow like Karen's Mum. An ambulance had been called and was on its way. After being checked over thoroughly at the hospital, they found no injuries apart from a half-inch gash just above my left eye. Nobody could understand how, from where I had fallen, I'd managed to twist and get myself in the position I had been in and how I'd ended up where I did; it was a mystery. We were asked several times if we were certain I fell where we said I did and asked if we were not mistaken, but we weren't. I had four stitches in my eyelid, and it had to stay bandaged for a week. Both Karen and I couldn't believe it and the very next day happily walked arm in arm together around the flats, her right eye and my left eye balancing each other out. Nobody believed us when we told them, it was too incredible to believe and too much of a coincidence.

I had felt nothing on my way down, as if I had fallen and was caught in a cotton wool ball. I didn't recall slipping; it was as if I had fallen asleep during my descent, not even feeling my eye hit the step. My head didn't hit anything on the way down to knock me out, as there was nothing to hit… just an empty space where everything I desired resides. I had laughed so much that day, there was no resistance in me, and I was open and flowed with the energy and, from that place, had become one with my desire in the empty space that lives between.

◊ ◊ ◊ ◊

Sure-footed as a goat Reflections

During school holidays and at weekends I woke up happy and excited for every new day. Whether it was raining, windy, snow or sun, I would utilise these gifts of nature and unite with whatever force was out that day to help and assist in the creation of adventures and new experiences.

The desire was so strong to have a bandage over my eye like my friend that, in that desire and the laughter of the day, I brought to me the very elements needed for that desire to manifest.

My Mum and Dad were always willing to assist in shaping my creations, supplying me with the tools and essential materials for me to bring them to life. I noticed how many other parents did not get involved and even tried to dissuade on many occasions, almost blocking the creative flow instead of encouraging it.

As I was climbing up the stairs before my fall, Karen had spoken about her fear of going to get her cyst cut out. I believe this lowered my very high vibration as I met her fear and tried to reassure her it would be ok. The next moment I was at the bottom of the steps. Would I have fallen if I had remained in a high vibration, and had the level drop allowed me to fall? I believe my soul took me step by step towards what was wanted, causing me no pain, just leading me impulse by impulse to the desired outcome.

I know it was divinely inspired as I had no marks or bruises other than the cut on my eye. I hit nothing and felt nothing, not even the cut. We were so tired after our day of fun; I suppose you could say it's possible I was so tired that I shut my eyes for a moment before falling. Anything is possible but I know for sure there are only meaningful coincidences and the physical reality was that the desire for a bandage on my eye was so strong it had manifested the very same day, as I had spoken it.

As children we are open to miracles, we expect, we see beauty everywhere, we get excited about little things, we are adventurous and full of wonder and our hearts are pure. We are conditioned by those around us into feeling less than we really are, instead of believing we are more than we can see. I would now like to take you to an experience where I got out of the way and allowed my inner light to work a miracle through me. This experience is called 'Dragonfly'…

Dragonfly

Sitting at my kitchen window, staring way up into the light blue sky, there were no clouds to be seen and it looked like it was going to be a nice warm day. I noticed the dancing particles seemed to have a pulse behind them. It was strange, and it was as though the sky had a heartbeat today. An image of Julius appeared, and I smiled; he was such a happy, generous soul. We had worked together for many years at the business centre, me as office manager and Julius as head of security. We instantly got on. We shared the same sense of humour and I'd grown fond of his honest and trustful nature. He would always go out of his way to help if he could and often went above and beyond his duties as security. Before my time there had been a fire in one of the offices at the business centre and he had risked his life, putting it out before the firemen came. The building was old and very wooden and that night he'd saved its life. It was not part of who he was to sit back and just allow the flames to take over.

It was the final goodbye today, with his body being laid to rest in the ground at the cemetery. Nobody likes a funeral, but I really didn't like them. It's not that I felt sad for the person being buried as I didn't, I had come to know they were not dead but just changing form, heading into a different dimension and releasing the burdens they carried around with them in this world. Their bodies were left to turn to dust in the ground but the bigger and best part of them, their essence, completely merging and being at one again with divine light. It was the pain and emotions from the people grieving I could feel that affected me, their feelings of loss and the tone of their cries touching and connecting with me in a dance of pain. I recalled the time I had gone to a funeral with a friend who just needed me with him for support. I didn't know the man that died, it had been a sudden and brutal death, and I was just there to comfort, but the amount of pain I felt from so many was so overwhelming I cried all the way through, my friend having to comfort me.

My daughter Lydia and I cuddled as we stood by the grave, watching the coffin being lowered. I knew he wasn't there; the bigger and best part of him was not in that box. The thought sent warmth through my heart and the warmth grew as I imagined him now healthy, happy and laughing again. I looked up in the sky to see the dancing particles and wondered if he was now one of them. A dragonfly hovered back and forth right over the grave; it stayed throughout our time there. It seemed to want to be part of the service as if, somehow, belonging with us and I nudged Lydia to show her.

After saying our goodbyes Lydia and I headed home, then, part of the way we separated, going in different directions. It had turned out to be a lovely, warm afternoon just as I'd expected, and I felt comfortable in my black, loose blouse and trousers, just perfect for this weather, I thought. As I walked, I noticed the road was busy with parents and children coming from school, the road was alive, a hive of activity and noisy with laughter and yelling, as the children excitedly headed home.

My mind was running over the day, the service, the chats I had with people, my daughter and the dragonfly. I was pondering and processing as I walked, when I realised I had walked up a road parallel to the road I normally walk up. The road I was on took me out of my way by about 5 minutes. It didn't make sense to me, I never use this road, and it's longer and less scenic. I was clearly operating on autopilot as my mind was elsewhere, but why would it take me out of my way? Never mind. It wasn't worth turning back now so I continued on.

My heart felt light, not how I'd felt so often at other funerals I'd been too. My ideas about death had changed and I had learnt not to absorb the pain of others. I had learnt how to have compassion, not empathy, in over-standing the pain, and not understanding and becoming one with it. I had also learnt the power of using the energy in my words as a means of comfort when fully aligned with source. As I reached the corner and turned into my road I crossed into the middle of the road and was shaken out of my peaceful thoughts by the scene I immediately came face-to-face with. Not two metres away, and heading straight at me, was a young man, no shirt on, with four young men behind him. My eyes quickly flicked from image to image… he was bleeding, face swollen and bloody, blood on his chest, which could be from injuries to his chest or blood from his face and head. The guy just behind him had a hammer in his hand, already raised, and the others had batons and a knife.

The bleeding man was stumbling and losing his balance, his adrenaline escaping from his injuries and had starting to give up, knowing how close they were. Our eyes met and the connection was made, and we ran towards each other. The man just behind him, his face all contorted, was ready to place the fatal blow to his head. There was no thought process, I didn't think, there was no time, so I got out of the way and let spirit move me. He collapsed in my arms, almost with an inner knowing he was safe. I put my left hand on the chest of the man with the hammer and looked him dead in the eyes as a "NO" travelled up from my solar plexus to my throat. I felt it erupt and smash into tiny particles as it left my mouth, connecting with him. At the very same time I felt the intensity of its power as it travelled along my arm, bursting through the skin of my palm, its energy connecting fully with his chest. Everything happened so fast but, in that moment, it was as if the movie had been paused, everything stopped in its tracks. All focus was on this connection. Then it all started again a moment later as play was pushed. The contorted face loosened, the hammer was lowered, and they all turned and ran off down the road the way they had come. The young man suddenly became heavy and, as we were in the middle of the road, we stumbled over to the pavement and I lay him down as others quickly gathered to assist. He had a stab wound in his back, so I lay him on his front and put his t-shirt, that had been tucked into his trouser belt, over it. The ambulance was quick to arrive and, once safely with the medics, I headed home. I washed my blood-stained hands, made myself a cup of tea and felt the need to sit in my garden. My little dog Pablo jumped up at me, sensing something was wrong, wanting to comfort me.

As I sat there, I was running through what just happened, going over it frame by frame as if I was replaying a specific part in a movie, back and forward trying to get as much from it as possible. I wanted to cry but couldn't. I hadn't felt any adrenaline; all the time it was happening I had felt completely calm and controlled. Now thoughts were swirling through my mind. It didn't matter to me who was right or wrong, what the young man did or didn't do, Or how they had felt justified to act like that. There was no judgement either way. The behaviour was caused because they had forgotten where they come from and who they really are.

Sitting there, I wondered, if it had been one of the other young men caught up in that situation, would it have been the same outcome? Would I have been strategically placed to assist? I know there is an abundance of assistance from higher consciousness, and I also know we are given free will to make our choices. Unless we ask for help and guidance, this higher consciousness does not interfere. Had this young man called out for help like I had done in the past? I received a thought: not just one life was saved, but all five of them. Had they managed to get him, whether intentionally or not, would they have killed him, taking his life and compromising their own? Instead of life sentences, this gave them an opportunity to grow and evaluate their lives, another chance to readjust their emotions and make changes…. I really hoped it did. I was amazed at how I had managed to stop that from happening. How had one person been enough? But, of course it was enough, it didn't come from me, it came through me. I realised I had taken the long route home so I could be placed in the right place at the right time, divinely orchestrated with perfect timing. All I had to do was get out of the way and follow the impulses, the gentle nudge from my creator to my inner light.

As I sat breathing deeply, a beautiful dragonfly appeared, it went back and forth several times in front of me, making sure I saw it, and then disappeared. In all the years I have lived here I had never seen one before and wondered if it was the same dragonfly as the one at the graveyard and if it was Julius, saying goodbye in his own special way. It is said that if a dragonfly visits and takes time to be near you it is important, as their lives are very short. They symbolise change, transformation, adaptability and self-realisation. It possesses the power of light, and learning through experiences. As we absorb the light, it teaches, guides and shines through us so others are drawn to it. The dragonfly serves to remind us that we, too, can reflect the light in a darkened world by letting the light shine through us.

Dragonfly reflections

In me getting out of the way and allowing source energy to flow through me, a miracle took place that day. Thinking about the spirit of Julius on my way home allowed me to be a vibrational match to the assistance being asked for by that young man.

Not only the injured man and the men chasing him, but also the many people and children on that road that would have been negatively affected by that fatal blow, had it taken place.

We must stay conscious and not allow a moment of anger to get the best of us; these moments can completely change our lives. Life as we know it can change in the blink of an unconscious eye.

I know wholeheartedly that there was a connection between the dragonfly at the grave side and the one I saw in my garden after the incident, but was it the same dragonfly? I couldn't be sure it was, but what I am sure of is, after leaving the graveyard that day I felt the spirit of Julius still with me. I am not a believer in coincidences and seeing both dragonflies was no coincidence, but a meaningful incident.

When we come into the world of form we are still so connected to the divine light and energy source, we have no resistance and just let it flow to and through us. As babies we know when we are hungry, tired or uncomfortable and let it be known to our caregivers, but as we grow, we are conditioned into thinking, feeling and behaving in a way that suits others. We quickly learn to forget our powers and abilities as our experiences with pain block the natural flow of divine energy that is always flowing to us, and we let fear take the lead in our lives.

I would like to take you to a time when I was small and still living in the flow of life, a time when I just allowed the flow of universal energy to take me to a place I'd never been before, allowing me to rise higher than I ever thought possible. This experience is called 'Sailors of the Sky'…

Sailors of the Sky

All my life I craved freedom. I was at my happiest running jumping and dancing around barefoot on the grass, soaking up the energy of the earth through my feet, and the feeling of the grass tickling my soul was heavenly. On this particular day, I was lying on my back on the grass just outside my balcony, looking up at the sky. It had been a glorious, sunny day and I had played all day. It was now late afternoon and the sun was at its friendliest, the powerful bright yellow had now turned into a beautiful soft, warm orange glow. I was moving the palms of my hands gently over the blades of grass, the uneven levels of each blade creating sensations all over my palms as I moved them back and forth. I looked up at the golden particles in the sky and asked, "What shall we do now?" I received no impulse, so remained where I was. I noticed some birds had appeared in the sky above and I watched them soaring and gliding above me. I could tell, even from far away, what birds they were by how they flew. We had been given a bag of books by a neighbour; they were about nature and animals. I loved all of them but was instantly drawn to the bird and the horse books. The connection was felt straightaway, as if we had known each other before. I loved reading all about them and this is where my love for them grew and grew. I learnt all about the different species of birds and received such pleasure from knowing what they were when I saw them flying around. I always seemed to find injured birds, or maybe they always found me, especially in early summer, just after the babies left the nest and were finding their wings. I'd pick them up carefully and take them home. We would hunt around for a small box to put them in, and Dad would help us make them a cosy home to nestle in. We kept them on the balcony, giving them water and bread dipped in milk to eat.

Sometimes they survived. It felt so good to watch them fly away, knowing you had helped keep them safe. Sometimes a rest was all they needed, but other times they didn't make it, their little souls flying away, soaring higher than ever before. Looking at its little limp body I wondered where the light in its eyes went, those little eyes that had been so alive, no longer curious, watchful and full of life.

This day, as I lay on the grass watching the birds, I noticed a seagull gliding so gracefully just above me. It looked so peaceful, not a care in the world. It was just flowing and being carried along by the breeze; I was completely mesmerised by it. I couldn't feel any wind and thought there must be a movement of air higher up and, just like the ocean, the sky had currents that weren't felt by us on the ground, and it fascinated me the more I thought about it.

I wondered if the seagull could see or feel the golden particles and wondered if they were playing together on the unfelt breeze. I had a burning desire to join them, Oh, how I wished I could fly, to experience what it felt like to glide with the wind and look down on the earth.

My seagull had been joined by another and I continued watching as they played and swerved just above me, sometimes just missing each other by inches, and the noise they made sounded just like laughter. I giggled as I watched them having fun and it seemed as though they were enjoying my focused attention and were revelling in the pleasure they were giving me, swooping even lower and closer to me. I wanted, with all my heart, to join them as I watched, completely mesmerised. I stayed focused for so long I could no longer move, it became so intense I felt like I was in a hypnotic trance. My peripheral vision completely disappeared and suddenly I felt like I was floating, as if I had just become particles. It felt like a part of me had escaped from the confines of my body, surpassing matter as the frequencies of my soul mingled with the playfulness of the seagull uniting and becoming one. The feeling was so intense I must have closed my eyes because, when I opened them, I saw life from above, a bird's eye view, and I gasped out loud as my new world suddenly became clear… my house, the big expanse of grass, the children playing near the football pitch. I could see people walking, the lady with her dog, and I laughed out loud as I saw Mrs Wright hanging out Sharon's underwear on her washing line. I felt the wind on my face and lowered my lids a little to protect my eyes. I was lifted higher as my wings caught an updraft of air and, in another moment, lowered again as it subsided. I was playing with the other seagull, swooping and diving in and out of the clouds, and I could see the golden particles all around me as we flowed and played. I had never felt like this before, the freedom was exhilarating, my heart was wide open and I felt so light and full of joy.

Somewhere in the background I could hear a faint sound, like a dull echo and, as its ripple got nearer and louder, I could hear my name being called. I looked down and was suddenly shocked to see myself lying on the grass, smiling. A second later I was abruptly brought back down to Earth by my Mum calling me. I felt a bit shaky, and it took me a few moments to resettle my perspective. What had just happened?? I sat up and looked up at the sky. There was only one bird now, he circled once making the laughing sound and then flew off behind the building. I shakily got to my feet and ran towards the balcony excitedly saying, "MUM, I WAS A BIRD! I was actually a bird, I was really flying in the sky!" Mum looked at me; she had been calling me for ages. I told her again, "Can you believe it Mum! I was a bird!" Mum was used to me. She had watched me be a tree before, and my bike was always a horse, so she acknowledged my accomplishment without question whilst picking the grass out of my hair.

I wasn't aware, back then, that the seagull represents freedom and independence, and they are seen as the sailors of the sky. There were many more things that we couldn't see, there were currents and streams of air that pushed and pulled, lifted and lowered the birds. We couldn't feel or see them from our viewpoint but, just because we couldn't see them, didn't mean they weren't there. Lying on the grass that day, I had either imagined it so well that it became real in those moments or, I had somehow managed to connect energetically with the bird, becoming one with it. Whatever happened, I would never be the same again, as I knew I had tapped into an unseen part of me and flowed in the undercurrents and updrafts of its stream.

Sailors of the Sky reflections

As children we are so open to possibilities, we can, and often do, tap into the realms of what is possible beyond our limited vision. We teach our children to be real and focus on the world around them instead of the one they are here to create, taking away their vision and potential to see they are much more than they can even imagine.

We could come up with reasons for why I experienced this. I could have fallen asleep and was dreaming of being a seagull. I could have imagined it so well it became real to me in that moment, or the one I chose to believe is with my desire so strong and the complete surrender to the delightful encounter I was enjoying with the birds, I had somehow got out of the way of myself and my body and became a part of the stillness where we are all connected and are all one.

The next experience I'd like to share with you is similar in energy, but this time I am grown, I am aware and fully conscious of the connection between myself and animal. This taught me that there is a universal language with no barriers that speaks to every living being and this vibrational frequency resonates with love and appreciation. There is no living thing that will not be affected by it. I'd like to share my story with you. It's called 'Powerful Spirit'…

Powerful Spirit

Before our trip to Costa Rica, Tracie and I had spoken about a dream we both shared of riding a horse along a beach, and now the dream was about to come true. Stacey told us about a particular riding place she had visited where the horses were loved, treated and embraced for the spiritual beings they were.

We had booked in advance to make sure this dream came true and the day before we were due to go it rained nearly all day. We knew they would cancel our ride if it continued, as the horses were not taken out in it. Our time in Costa was almost over so there was no time to reschedule and, with more heavy rain forecast for tomorrow, there was nothing else to do but sit, visualising riding the horses on the beach in the sun tomorrow.

Up early, I met the sunrise with a smile as I sat there, eagerly anticipating its arrival. It was a glorious morning and as we set off, I sat in the back of the car with the windows open and the breeze blowing through. The noise of the wind meant I couldn't hear the words being spoken so I shut my eyes, allowing the wind to whip my hair in my face. The wind produced an excitement in me, it always had. The way the wind felt while I was sitting in the car as it moved around me, searching and scanning me before moving on, and then another would arrive, never the same particles of air, always changing, flowing and moving. I recalled watching westerns as a child, the native Indians bareback-riding with the wind blowing in their faces, so completely free. I recalled how I had wanted to be one, so had my big sister Caz. She had wanted to be a Shashawnee. I don't think it was the tribe especially she liked, but more the enjoyment she got from saying the name, and she said it often.

It would make me so angry watching the Indians being tricked out of their land and how unfairly they were treated. Something inside me deeply resonated with their way of life and I loved hearing the truth and wisdom in the stories told by the elders as they spoke about the Great Spirit.

I pulled the window up a bit to become more present with my friends. We were going to ride through the rainforest with all its wonderful offerings until we reached the beach. How perfect would that be? I knew this offered an incredible experience and expected nothing but the most thrilling ride of my life.

As we pulled up and got out, I felt the familiar excitement rise up in my stomach. It continued upwards, trying to escape through my mouth but, as usual, my throat stopped its flow. Our horses were waiting for us, unsaddled, under the canopy sheltered from the sun. I smiled at their freedom and felt a peaceful, loving vibe and instantly felt at ease. There were two dark brown ones and one speckled grey and I knew instinctively which one was mine and asked our friendly guide Fabio for confirmation. My horse was a mare called Sanice, meaning 'Grey'. I felt the connection instantly as I'd lived my life between the darkness and light and the colour of my horse felt perfectly in tune with me.

Whilst Fabio prepared and saddled up the other horses, I got acquainted with her. I knew she couldn't understand my English words telling her how beautiful she was and how blessed I felt for her allowing me to ride her, but I knew for sure she could feel them. She listened to my tone and felt the love coming through my hands as they ran over her body, her head, and ears and under her mane. For a while I only felt the love flowing from me, but soon began to feel the ebb and flow of connection as the vibration came back and we both stood there basking in the moment. She looked around at me with her big, soulful eyes, and a deeper connection was made.

I spoke to her, asking her to be patient with me as I wasn't an experienced rider like the others. I had only been on a pony once before... it had been on a holiday in Wales with my family. It was the one thing I had wanted to do. It was a half-day trek across the moors, both my sisters and I went. My brother was too young at the time, so he stayed behind with Mum and Dad. We were told we had been assigned the ponies that most matched our personalities. I had wondered, at the time, why that pony had been chosen for me as both my sisters were given calm, relaxed ponies, whilst I was given one that could be a bit mischievous and was known occasionally to nip at the other ponies.

We had made our way across the moors, each pony happily following the one in front with no problems, but as we reached the town to stop for lunch, my pony nipped the pony my younger sister Dee was on and it reacted, throwing her off. Dee's foot got caught in the stirrup and she was dragged along as it trotted away. Thank God Dee was unhurt; she was a little shaken up but bravely got back on. After that incident my pony and I were shunned and told to stay at the back. Looking back, I realised why that pony had been picked for me. I understood him, he could be a bit mischievous when bored but really didn't mean any harm, he was only playing.

As we saddled up, Fabio, being aware of our riding abilities, asked me if I'd feel comfortable at some point in the journey to try a trot and canter, and I said I definitely would, and we set off. We came to a gate that led into a field where horses were roaming freely, some of them coming up to nuzzle with our horses as we rode through, and Fabio laughed as some naughty ones used it as an opportunity to escape into a larger field. He said it was ok, they would be called back later. It was so special; I couldn't stop smiling.

As we rode through the rainforest, I was in awe at the smells and the sounds of nature. I loved the way the sun found its way through the gaps in the trees, shining its beams of light onto sections of the forest, highlighting and uncovering any darkness. It looked and felt magical. There were small streams we waded through along the way and, all the time, I kept stroking my girl's neck, telling her how beautiful she was, and she began responding by pulling her neck back to see me, in confirmation that she understood. Fabio was very experienced with both horses and nature and told us about the trees and what each of them does for the forest. He told us about the birds and the animals that lived there, and I found it all so interesting. Whilst in Costa I had been inspired to look up the spiritual significance of each species of bird we encountered, and his eyes lit up as I told Fabio the ones I could remember and said that perhaps this was another thing he could bless the people he guided with.

Wading through the small stream and inlets of the forest, I recalled my first encounter with a horse. It was when the rag-and-bone man came plodding along our street, shouting, "Any old iron, any old iron," and people would come out, bringing old furniture or clothes they no longer wanted, and he'd stop to pile it up on the cart. I looked lovingly at the tired horse with his head down, blinkers on, and daydreamed about riding him along the plains and up to the mountain top where we would stop and look over, my hair and his mane blowing in the wind. The rag-and-bone man started coming every fortnight and would stop and have a pint or two at the Enterprise pub on the corner, leaving his horse outside. As soon as I knew he was there, I'd stop playing, excitedly telling my friends, "Let's go see the horse," but they weren't interested and told me it's only a dusty old cart horse. I would run to my Mum asking for a carrot, apple or anything a horse eats, and she would always find me something.

The rag-and-bone man knew I'd turn up and he would roll his eyes and shake his head as I'd tell him I would look after Shining Star while he was inside. I'd renamed him as 'Ned' didn't suit him. He enjoyed carrots, but apples were his favourite. He would peep at me through the gaps in the blinkers as I talked to him and stroked him under his mane and along his forehead and my hand would be covered in dirt. My Mum had a soft hairbrush that she used on our hair. One day I sneaked it out so I could give him a good brush. I could tell he really loved it, as his tail kept swishing from side to side. To this day I don't know which of us was the lucky one who that got his dirt brushed into our hair that night. I smiled at the thought of him, yes, he was dusty, very dusty, and old, but he was beautiful to me.

Coming out of my daydream I thought how hot and humid it was and just as I thought it, so it started to rain. It trickled through the trees, leaving its droplets of cool water all over us. It wasn't enough to prevent us going on, but just enough to refresh us and our horses, and it was so needed and appreciated. The universe had responded to my thought and provided the answer even before I knew the rain was a desire. Approaching the clearing, I could see the beach in the distance, just behind the canopy of trees and foliage, and could hear the familiar sounds of the waves as they pushed themselves onto the sand. As we came through the trees it was like riding out into a different world, leaving the safety and closeness of the jungle and suddenly being birthed onto the largest open expanse of beach I'd ever seen, and I took in the new sounds and smells of this new world as my eyes adjusted to the light. It felt like we had just discovered a new part of the world. The sand was fresh and new with no marks left behind by those that had gone before. We were all alone, just us, our horses and the beach.

The feeling of joy rose up from my stomach, this time my throat no longer holding it back, and let out a loud noise sounding like a Native American Indian war cry. Everyone laughed and joined in as we all rode along the beach, whooping with joy. I was in ecstasy; life couldn't get much better than this. Looking over my shoulder to where we had just emerged through the trees, the forest, the red macaws flying past, it looked and felt like I was in a beautiful dream. As the sea waves gently hit the legs of my horse, splashing sea water over my feet, that moment arrived in me again where I felt the beautiful, intense connection to every living thing. The pure bliss was overwhelming, and I allowed the emotion to fill up my eyes, the state of pure love threatening to trickle down my face. Tracie and I looked at each other, connecting with both eyes and soul. Her eyes were full. She felt it too.

Fabio asked if I was ready to have a canter, and I was, so he explained what I needed to do. Speaking softly to Sanice, I asked her to be careful with me, I hadn't done this before, and that I was nervous. I also apologised in advance for anything I may do in my inexperience that causes her any discomfort. I told her I was in good hands and would surrender and allow it to happen. She heard me, loud and clear, and her head came round to look at me, assuring me that she had me.

We started trotting, then went into a canter. I relaxed, surrendering to her, my body, mind and soul allowing her the room to express. She felt the freedom, she wanted to run and went into a full-on gallop. I couldn't believe it; I was galloping along a beach in Costa Rica, completely at one with my horse, living my dream. The wind had decided to join us, all three enjoying and sharing the movement and oneness of the ride.

I suddenly became conscious that I had never ridden this fast before and became aware of the others behind me and felt it was time to slow down and stop. No noise was made; it was a thought that turned into a feeling that was felt by my horse. The connection between us so strong, she slowed down and then stopped, taking a look round at me, and I swear she was smiling at me through her eyes. I laughed as I stroked her beautiful neck, thanking her as the others reached me, and we all laughed as the feeling of pure exhilaration erupted in us. Fabio was only supposed to take us out for an hour and a half but was enjoying our energy and enthusiasm so much he decided to lengthen it. We walked along the beach, soaking in the day and enjoying each and every moment.

On reflection later that night, I wondered where my connection with horses came from. The books I'd been given as a child triggered it, but surely it had to be there already to be reached. Even before the books I was given on horses, my bike had never just been a bike, it was always a horse, so acting on an impulse to search deeper I looked up the spiritual meaning of a horse and it started to make sense…The horse is a symbol of Freedom, travel, movement and desire. In Native

American tribes they represent power. The horse has a naturally wild and powerful spirit and always wants to break free. It is said they represent a journey…

I had been on this journey all my life, desiring freedom and wanting to break free. The wind was always present in my dreams and visions, representing excitement and movement and I was beginning to remember my true power. In that beautiful flow of surrender, me, my horse and the wind became one that day and the powerful and peaceful Indian Chief looked down and smiled as we played.

Powerful Spirit reflections

Tracie and I had spoken about riding horses along a beach and in our visualisations, we could see it and feel it, and in that feeling our dream manifested into physical form. We realised that our dreams, however vivid, real and pleasurable, always exceeded our expectations when they materialised.

The weather forecast more rain for next day and we were running out of time to live out this dream, so I visualised the outcome I wanted and, in that visualisation and expectation, changed the outcome.

I remember having a really strong connection to Native American Indians as a child. I felt the injustice deeply, almost personally, and as a child really wanted to let them know we were not all like those that represented us.

It was only when the fearful thought arrived in my mind, making me aware of my riding abilities, that I felt the emotion of limitation and the need to stop, but there were really no limits, they were only my thoughts as I had already surpassed them and was riding my horse and galloping along the beach.

My horse could not understand me verbally, but clearly understood the energy and frequencies given out. We connected energetically, transcending any barriers or limitations.

Fabio, our guide, was so intoxicated by our energy, he didn't want the feeling to end and we continued on for much longer.

This was a dream come true and the experience was so much better than the imagined event. I had always had a real connection with animals; they are instinctive and have to feel their way through life, using every part of their senses to be aware of any danger. I have found them to be very receptive to the frequency your heart is emitting and would love you to come with me to the next experience. This one is called 'Dolphins'…

Dolphins

On the way to visit with the dolphins, both Lisa and I were really disappointed to find out we were in fact going to an enclosed space right near the sea, as we were under the impression we were to be taken out to sea where we could swim with dolphins that were free. I thought about how that must be for the dolphins, being so close to freedom, teasing them, their desire growing more and more each day. Everything they could ever want or need was just a few metres away. They could smell it, they could even see it; it was so very close. I sighed deeply and thought how wonderful it would be for them to be physically free again, to experience the pure joy of jumping out of the water for no other reason than wanting to. The coach took twists and turns along the mountain roads, and I watched people going about their daily tasks and wondered what their lives were like. I noticed how green and lush the land and trees looked. It had been raining earlier so nature, having taken its shower, was still moist and looking fresh and clean.

I looked up at the sky. It was a deep blue, and I was pulled in by its depth and mesmerised by its beauty. I noticed tiny little birds way up high playing, gliding and soaring on the currents, and began thinking how alike the sky was to the sea. The birds could have been fishes swimming in an ocean of deep blue, each one, both so vast, deep and mysterious. I wondered why some people are so drawn to being in a boat in the middle of the ocean, (something that never appealed to me). Perhaps it put everything into perspective, being such a small object surrounded by blue.

I hadn't completely finished my thoughts when the coach pulled into the parking area and everyone started grabbing bags and coats and bustling to get off. I was in no hurry; the excitement of the destination had faded once I knew the details of our trip. We had paid in advance, making sure we got to experience swimming with the dolphins in Mexico and, although disheartened, I knew everything in life was an experience and experience teaches.

As we were taken through the safety measures, the do's and don'ts, and put our life jackets on, we were told under no circumstances must we touch the dolphins. I didn't think it could get any worse but after hearing that, it did. As we entered the first enclosure, the heaviness in the air weighed me down mentally and physically and, at that point, I wasn't sure if it belonged to me or the beautiful dolphins swimming around. The enclosures were their natural environment. It was at the edge of the sea, with sea water, rocks, everything you would expect, but closed off from the sea and its vastness, and so far from the clean blue pool you see at Marine World. We were instructed to get into the water and swim to the middle and allow the dolphins to come to us and were reminded once again not to touch them. Once in the middle, we separated about an arm's length from each other so they could swim between us. They swam around, then in-between us, checking each of us out slowly. I knew they could sense things. I'd read and heard so many wonderful stories about them.

As I floated in the water watching them, admiring the way they moved and glided with such ease, I was suddenly overcome with emotion. I felt love welling up in me until I was full to bursting point, my heart having no option but to open up, sending ripples of love into the water. As they passed me, one by one they would turn on their side to get a good look at me, making sure we made eye contact and taking time to connect. This one dolphin, the largest of the group, brushed past me making sure I felt not just his presence but also his strength. As our eyes met a feeling of overwhelming emotion rose up in me. I couldn't make it out at first, it wasn't the same feeling of love I'd felt a moment ago. It was welling up from the pit of my stomach, up through my chest and travelling up where it was caught by my throat... I wanted to scream out loud in frustration and for freedom, but it was too large and remained a lump that I couldn't release or swallow.

My heart, wide open, had caught and translated the frequency they sent to me, and I was sure now that the feeling of heaviness I'd encountered when entering the enclosure was their vibration I was picking up on. It had also became mine now, connected mentally, physically and emotionally, we were as one. There were about five of us in our group and as I looked around, I thought the others seemed unaware of what was happening on a deeper level and suddenly became annoyed at their apparent lack of awareness, as they were smiling and enjoying themselves. I caught myself becoming conscious of my thoughts, remembering not all thoughts become words, some are felt but never spoken and I shouldn't assume anything.

They had stopped swimming around us and seemed taken by a young woman. They were circling her and the smaller dolphins were nudging her with their bodies. I have to admit to feeling a slight tinge of jealousy rise up in me, like a small wave hitting the shore, but it left a few seconds later with the outgoing tide as I observed them. I asked the woman if she was pregnant and she confirmed she was three months along and remarked that although she wasn't showing, they seemed to know. I can remember feeling so much love for those beautiful dolphins in that moment and feeling silly for my wave. They knew life was being formed and were fascinated. They wanted to embrace this new life with happiness and wonder, despite wanting to scream out loud for their freedom.

The supposed highlight of the trip was being pulled along by a harness attached to a dolphin. "You keep your feet up and flat and you will be pulled along the enclosure," shouted the instructor. Whilst waiting for my turn I thought of the groups of waiting people that these precious dolphins had to do that with, day in and day out, and felt no pleasure when my turn came. I realised I should have refused, as my thoughts about becoming a part of it all and participating completely lowered my vibration.

At the second enclosure we got into the water separately, to have a picture taken with one of the dolphins kissing your cheek. I was first to get in and received a wet, salty kiss and, as I stood watching, the dolphin started to refuse to kiss people. I knew it was fed up and tired, it was dreaming about the freedom of the sea and that inward scream returned.

As we headed toward the exit, Lisa and I looked at each other with a knowing that we both felt the same way. We were told we could purchase the pictures at the desk on our way out, but it was bad enough having the images and emotions ingrained in my memory, never to be erased. I didn't need the physical reminder as well, so I opted out. Lisa said aloud, "No thanks, I don't want to be reminded of our visit to unhappy dolphins." She made a slight smile appear on my face. She had always said what she felt and I really liked her for that. A couple of instructors were waiting at the exit to say goodbye and to wish us a safe journey back. I was suddenly drawn to the one on my right and positioned myself to meet him. I stopped, looking him straight in the eye, the way the dolphin had done to me and, clasping his hand in a sandwich-like grip with both hands, I said, "They are so unhappy and screaming to be free." I felt a connection, a recognition. He knew, he felt it too. He didn't utter a word, just bowed his head once in acknowledgment of our connection and gave my hand a gentle squeeze before releasing it. Walking back to the coach I looked around, feeling the energy of his focus and our eyes met once again. My eyes filled up as the feeling in the pit of my stomach returned.

On the way back Lisa turned to me and told me she didn't enjoy one moment of that, and we chatted about how it made us both feel. As we settled into the journey my heart was still heavy with desire for freedom as I looked up at the deep blue sky and continued watching the birds way above me. I knew it would take a while to release the emotion I had taken in from the dolphins and re-centre myself again. The animal kingdom, nature, had always assisted with my growth and I had become a master at feeling like I was in two worlds at the same time, having one foot in each, and could step from one to the other from the stillness and focus of my mind. The dolphins helped me to see that the outward and inner journey are really one, there is no separation, everything is energy that constantly flows to and through me. I choose to feel the connection consciously, or choose to resist, but the choice is always mine.

Looking back into the sky from my window seat I continued watching the birds as they began diving and playing, and I imagined they were the dolphins roaming and jumping for joy, freedom tasting both salty and sweet, and felt the rising of my vibration as I realised the power of my thoughts. I could do nothing right now but my desire, my will and my love could transcend any barriers, any restrictions. I was not physically with them anymore but could still feel them; they were letting me know it was time for me to release old emotions no longer serving me. At the same time, I was letting them know they would feel the waves of the ocean sliding off their skins again as they jumped out of the water for no other reason but for pure joy. The accumulation of desire for freedom was strong and building day by day, as more and more people felt the connection and I relaxed knowing they already knew the two worlds I flitted to and from were also theirs.

In 2017, Mexico City banned dolphin captivity in their country after two failed attempts. The dolphins that were in captivity at the location we visited were to be re-homed, rehabilitated and then reintroduced, allowing them to live out the rest of their lives in Peace.

Dolphins reflections

This story shows how a desire for freedom became so strong that it transcended any barriers. Language was no longer a thing to overcome as the frequencies of feeling became the force. The energy took over completely, affecting everyone with the same vibration and, as that desire grew, uniting in intensity, it had no choice but to manifest into the physical realm.

Our thoughts are so powerful; they can literally take us down or make us rise. We have to be conscious of the thoughts we are thinking in every moment. Are you consciously choosing your thoughts or just allowing your mind to wander wherever it wants to go? Conscious focus is the key.

My vibration was low before I got to the enclosure, as my thoughts about the dolphins' captivity had lowered them, so I became a complete match to their vibration, and they could feel this. The large dolphin not only made sure we connected visually but had brushed me, making sure I felt its frustration for freedom and, as I connected with it, the vibration was translated as it travelled to my throat to be voiced as their pain.

I was appreciating the wonder and beauty of the dolphins when my heart opened up, pouring love into the water, and they felt these ripples of love. As I watched them, fascinated by the new life they could feel growing and forming inside the pregnant lady, I knew that, despite their discontentment with their environment, they could still see past it to give love and attention to the beautiful life being created.

It was not just the dolphins' desire but the growing accumulated desire for their freedom from others that had become co-operative components in bringing about the manifestation of their freedom.

This experience made me realise the power of the heart. Opening up and having the vibrations reach a living thing that doesn't speak the same language, but shares the same feelings, was a powerful insight. What was at first a painful experience soon became an incredible experience, as the components of the united desire lined up to bring it into physical manifestation. With this in mind, I want to take you to an experience my Dad had when he was in the army. He told this story to us through his eyes, but it was received by me through mine. It is called 'Army Ants'…

Army Ants

My Dad was a young boy of 15 years when he went into the army, and he came out a man of 20. He went from being a boy playing football in the street one minute, to leaving England and everyone he knew and loved behind to be sent over to fight in the jungles of Malaysia the next. Just like the others, he was completely unprepared for the horrors he would have to face, day in, day out, for the next five years. There were no practice runs, they were sent straight over. Many died from an unconscious awareness of their surroundings, the so-called enemy were more than other humans, there were life-threatening animals, insects, malaria and other diseases to contend with.

Strong bonds of friendship are created between people experiencing extreme conditions and environments. I could only imagine what it was like to be talking with a friend one minute, and the next he's dead with a bullet in his head. The pain and the emotions of terror he felt living on his nerves, minute by minute, must have been immense. Dad didn't speak about the horrors to us and didn't glorify killing. He would always leave that out of his stories. When I innocently asked him how many people he killed, he told me he just dodged the bullets. I could sense and sometimes see it in his eyes that he felt deeply regretful for having taken lives but, with nowhere to go with it, it remained inside him, casting a shadow that surfaced now and again in fearful thoughts of the world and everyone in it.

He was fully conscious now and the images of the lights that were blown out by his hands stayed in his heart. It troubled him and remained in a place that couldn't be reached or understood by us.

When he first arrived in Malaysia the unknown sounds of the animals and insects, along with the enemy around every corner, was terrifying. The jungle and everything in it was harsh at times, and nature had her own rules, but he soon found the beauty in the different life forms and the once unfamiliar sounds soon became a comfort, reminding him there was more life going on around him that he was currently experiencing.

He told us a story about one day, when they had settled down in a clearing to make camp. They were all tired. It had been an exhausting day and Dad was feeling really low as he'd lost a good friend. As they settled in a few of the guys were telling stories and laughing and, as he sat there, he could feel their laughter whirling around his head, creating a feeling of irritation and anger deep inside.

They were under strict orders that nobody was to stray from camp as they would become easy prey, but this day he didn't care. The heavy feeling wouldn't lift and he needed some time to be by himself. He had almost died from malaria and was still recovering. Today he was really low, depression trying hard to make a home in his head and to settle in. Having to be on high alert was taking a toll on his emotions, but he knew his life depended on it. He wondered what this was all about and was, at that point, tired of this life.

Slipping out of camp, he found himself a tree to sit under and started making a roll-up. The sounds of the jungle were comforting. There was life, and he could hear the monkeys and the different sounds of the bird calls. He tried to focus and really listen to them but was too full of questions, so he sat there smoking, one ear listening out for the answers, the other listening out for any unusual rustlings. As he pulled hard on the roll-up, taking the tobacco deep into his lungs, he noticed an army ant that had suddenly appeared and was heading towards him. They were known to be relentless and ravenous, killing and eating their victims mercilessly, so he looked around, making sure there were no more and, feeling no danger from this solo ant, he allowed it to walk up his leg and back down again. He watched as its large black body and its antennae moved in all directions independently. It seemed to be picking up the signals radiating from his leg. He knew it was dangerous to focus so intently on the ant, but gained some level of comfort from leaving the reality of his world behind, desperately needing to feel the space between the worlds that he'd come to know.

He watched it walk down to his ankle, disappearing for a second as it jumped off his boot onto the leaves, and continued watching as it picked up the pace and scurried off into the distance. He was surprised it hadn't taken a bite out of him and thought perhaps the ant knew today he didn't care. He lit up another roll-up and tried to find some peace from the questions and images playing on repeat, round and round in his head.

After a while he heard a slight noise in the distance. He couldn't make it out as it was unfamiliar, and it wasn't a firm movement but more of a flow, as if something was gliding along the surface of the leaves. All his senses kicked in and came alive all at once, he was on high alert. He looked in the direction it was coming from. Maybe it was a snake. No, it was larger than a snake, he thought. As he peered into the distance, he saw what looked like a carpet of shimmering black heading towards him. It was wide and long, and he'd never seen anything like it before. He slowly got up to his feet so he could run if need be and, as it came closer, he realised it was a sea of ants. It suddenly dawned on him the reason the ant hadn't bitten him, as it didn't want to alert him and had hurried back to tell the others he'd come across a victim.

My Dad hot-footed it back to camp as fast as he could and as he came to the clearing was suddenly really happy to see the others. He was greeted like a long, lost pal; they were happy to see him too. His best mate George had tried to convince him not to go but understood his need to be alone and had greeted his return with a mug of hot tea. As he sat down, he looked around the camp at his mates and quietly smiled as the jokes were thrown around the camp, the heaviness he had felt beginning to disappear more and more with each smile. He realised each man felt the same way, they just didn't speak about it. He had heard them in the quiet and stillness of the dark. They hid it behind their laughter and jokes, only allowing the releasing of tears to flow in the privacy of their beds at night.

His inner light, the essence of him, was still very much alive, and knowing what he needed had sent signals out to the universe, delivering the sea of ants. The choice was all his as to whether they consumed him or gave him his zest for life back.

Ants are an example to us of co-operation, diligence, devotion, organisation, hierarchy and system. He now knew he was just one of the army ants the system had created. He would have to be diligent, making sure his outer world didn't control his inner world, otherwise he would become just another victim of the shimmering black sea that would take him over and consume him.

The army ants were brought together as one scout went in search and, from the darkness of his mind, all his questions were answered. He knew there was great power in unity and no matter how bad things got, together they would make it through. He realised that the two worlds coincided simultaneously, and he could choose the world he wanted and, although one ear would always listen out for unusual rustlings, the other would focus on hearing the beauty and sounds of nature and the laughter of his friends.

◊ ◊ ◊ ◊

Army Ants Reflections

My Dad was only a teenager when he was sent over to the jungles of Malaysia to fight. With only basic training given, nothing could prepare him and many others for what they were about to experience. Taking other peoples' lives does impact you, despite it being deemed 'ok' because it's war.

There were no programs in place to help those that suffered with PTSD after the war was over; they were just supposed to settle back into normal life, with the images and experiences flashing back to them all the time.

My Dad made the sounds and sights of nature his escape from what he was living. By focusing on the things that gave him pleasure, he found relief from what was occurring around him.

With his vibration low and his tired thoughts about his life bringing him even lower, his questions were instantaneously answered, by taking his attention off the problems and re-focusing his attention on the ant. His soul, in unison with the universe, was quick to bring about the experience he needed to bring about his answers, and they all came in the form of the ants. Was he really tired of life? Was he so depressed that he no longer cared? The experience brought with it clarity and a new zest for life.

Situations like this can make us realise and appreciate what we have, even if it appears small and insignificant at the time. It's all about looking for the things to appreciate. If we look, we can find them everywhere and in every situation. It's important to appreciate all the things in your life and take nothing for granted as, the more you appreciate, the more you bring things into your life to appreciate.

Your mind is a powerful tool, and many have lost themselves to their mind, allowing it to control them to such a point, they no longer can see hope or appreciate what they have. Some might say, "…but his situation was real, death was happening all around him. Was he just supposed to pretend it wasn't happening?" And I say, the two worlds were happening simultaneously. Where the death and horror were, there was also life and birth happening. Be aware of both, but it's your choice what you focus your attention on. One will lower your vibration, showing you more, and the other will inspire you, taking you to new heights.

This story made me aware of the connection between our thoughts and what we bring into our reality, it stayed with me throughout my life and had a big impact on me. I saw and felt the way the universe delivered what Dad needed to pick himself up from his depressed state; it was ok to feel the discontent and question the needless killing that was going on around him, as this is what we are here to do, to question and to make changes, but once we have acknowledged it, we have to focus our attention on the solution and in transforming it. This now flows to a story called 'Perro'…

Perro

'Another beautiful day in Costa Rica!' was my first thought, smiling and stretching out of my meditation. It was so easy to meditate here. I just focused on the white noise of the insect orchestra and my mind cleared instantly.

Back home I liked to go to bed at around 11pm and get up at 6am, as I love the newness of the mornings and consciously welcoming the new day in. I loved to revel in the quietness before the hustle and bustle started but, since being in the rainforest, I found myself going to bed at 7pm and getting up half an hour before the Howler monkeys, around 3.30am. The monkeys had become my natural wake-up call, letting me know meditation time was over.

My bedroom window overlooked the jungle side of the house, and I could literally lie in bed watching the wildlife outside. I would watch as the black squirrels played with each other, scampering from tree to tree, in a game of tag along the branches of the tree just outside my window. The line of busy ants carrying large green leaves along the edge of the wall, with leaves so much bigger than the ant itself that, from a distance, they looked like they were walking along all by themselves. I put a large stick in the way of their route to see whether they would change their direction, but they just found another way around or over it. They were so focused on their mission that, by not focusing on the problem, they found the solution.

We slept with the windows open as it was too hot to close them and all that stood between me and the jungle was a piece of netting to prevent insects from getting in. In London I lived on the ground floor and wouldn't dream of sleeping with my window wide open, but here, despite the many species of animals freely roaming around, I felt no fear and even embraced it.

I woke up naturally around 3am every morning; I would quickly and quietly go to the toilet next door to my room, putting on the torch to see the floor as I walked. Stacey had given us a torch each to use in the dark, after all, we were in the rainforest - spiders, insects and scorpions were a common feature. We were the trespassers, this was their home and native Costa Ricans, Ticos as they were known, respected that. I loved the relationship they had with nature, it really touched me.

Heading out into the living space to put the pot on for a nice cup of tea, I smiled and thought some things never change. Here I am, in the jungle, and I still want my cuppa in the morning. So did Tracie, who appeared soon after the pot had boiled and as soon as it was made, we headed outside together to sit on the veranda to drink and soak up the morning vibe. Since our arrival we had bought and cooked our own meals, not wanting to be a burden to our friends and, in any case, both Tracie and I didn't eat any meat whilst Oliver and Stacey enjoyed a good steak.

It was time to go to the farmers' market in town to stock up again on fresh produce. There was no convenience store just minutes away, like in London. We had to drive half-way down a mountain and head into town for supplies. That morning, Oliver noticed the car was playing up and had taken it to get looked at; he had set off early and expected it to take most of the day as he had to wait for the car so he could get back.

Our food had completely run out and, not wanting to go without food all day, Tracie and I discussed walking down to the farmers' market. We knew it would be a very long trek down the mountain along the dirt track, but it was a beautiful day and, after all, how hard could it be? The more we spoke about it the more appealing it became, and the more adventurous we felt. It would do us good to go out on our own for a while. Since our arrival, we had been with either Oliver or Stacey at all times.

After getting showered and dressed, we headed to where Stacey was and found her on the veranda, exercising, one of her most favourite things to do. Stacey was not happy with our decision and suggested we wait until Oliver returns so he can drive us. We knew that could be all day and the market could be closed by the time he got back, and we literally had eaten our last bit of food. Our appetites had increased whilst we were here, the freshness of the food was so welcomed by our bodies, and they just seemed to crave more and more of the goodness on offer.

Stacey tried to convince us to wait. She said, "Nobody walks around here, it just isn't done," but the thought of fresh food, along with our adventurous spirits and the impulses received to go, spurred us on.

I felt no fear heading out. I'd slept with my windows open, and that's at night in the dark. It was light out now; there was no darkness. We walked along, chatting, excited to be out on our own and in one of the quiet moments I recalled our first meeting. We didn't know back then that it was to be the start of a great life adventure and a shared journey of enlightenment. We both had felt the loneliness of our paths, and both asked for someone that could not only see and feel the vision of creating a new Earth but someone that we could truly be ourselves with…. In Tracie I not only found my best friend, but I also found my soul sister. We had been friends a long time now, but never been away together, this being our first time. I'd been away with people before and you really do see another side to them when you're on holiday together, but Tracie and I just clicked even more, we flowed; it was as if all the layers of our human side were stripping away, leaving our lights to shine at their brightest.

As we walked along, we hadn't realised how far apart each neighbour was, if you could call them neighbours. In the car they had seemed much closer, there were 3 houses, and each must have been about half a mile apart. As we continued along, we noticed there was nothing but rainforest on either side of us, and nothing but dirt track in front or behind and, for a moment, we looked at each other telepathically, wondering if this was a good idea after all. We had a very brief discussion about what we would do if a wild animal came out of the jungle but, as reality dawned on us that there was nothing we could do and there was nowhere to go, we quickly changed the subject and re-focused our attention on the fresh food and new options we could find to try.

It had taken ages to get to the first house, despite it being all downhill. It was the house in process of being built, and its structure was in place but still in need of a lot of TLC. On our first day here, we had joked on our way up in the car that they were getting it prepared for us. As we approached and lined up with the fence at the front of the house, we were shocked out of our skin by a pack of ferocious dogs that suddenly appeared, looking at us and snarling through the gaps in the fence. There were about five of them, all different sizes. They didn't just seem to be warning us not to come too close, and they were extremely intimidating and aggressive.

Doing a quick assessment and taking mental pictures, the fence didn't look strong enough to hold them for long, and there were gaps everywhere, but even more troubling was the energy I felt coming from them. It was the energy I can only describe as a frenzied happiness that they had come across us. We were already aware there was absolutely nothing we could do if they got out and there was nowhere we could go. There were lots of trees but none we could climb; we were miles from anywhere, no houses around and not a soul in sight.

We both clasped each other in a hand grip as we began walking past and stepping up the pace. We were praying for help and talking about the fence and how angry the dogs were. Our happy vibration five minutes ago was replaced by fear that had taken us over, and was now feeding us, lowering our vibration. Quickly regaining some composure, we realised we had to get a grip, not on each other, but on our emotions, as we were feeding their excitement with our feelings of fear.

While the dogs continued barking and snarling, noses pushed

halfway through the fence, we knew we had to change it up. We had both been through so much in our lives and were at a stage where we understood the power of our thoughts and emotions and the impact they have in our outer world. We were on high alert so we began soothing ourselves with words. Looking at each other for comfort we spoke aloud asking our creator to send angels to help us. In an instant the noises the dogs were making changed. The frequency and intensity turned into a higher pitch as, all of a sudden, they left the fence. At the very same time the frequency changed I heard an audible voice, it spoke clearly and confidently with an added hint of excitement as one of the dogs said, "I know a way out, follow me," as they ran off alongside the fence. My gut did a somersault and I felt physically sick as I told Tracie they know a way out, I heard one of them say it, and we clasped each other's hands again for comfort. There was absolutely nothing we could do…but surrender fully to the moment and just be.

The gaping hole that stood between fear and love had to be filled in and quickly. I had been to this place before, so had Tracie; a place where time and things are no longer real, a place of pure surrender where nothing but space inside your mind exists, where you feel nothing but the energy inside you and all thought has dissolved away. When we spoke again, the words we sent out into the universe were not words of distress and desperation, it was the power of love that came flowing out of us. We had exchanged our thoughts of fear and danger to thoughts of love and miracles and began singing to raise our vibration as we walked.

We could still hear them as we reached the corner. Alongside the house was a little dirt track and, as we passed it, I looked down it to see the dogs, one by one, escaping from under the fence and heading up the hill towards us. I told Tracie and, for a brief second, we felt the seriousness of our situation again but brought our focus back in line quickly with the frequency of love, surrendering once again completely to the moment as we sent out ripples of love to every living thing on the planet and beyond.

I looked back down the dirt track. I had to. I had always had a fear of turning my back on what I feared, and I felt less afraid when I faced it. Somehow the knowing, however bad, was better than the unknown. They were all free and heading our way, but I had let go of the fear, as I'd done many times before and, as soon as a blink of my eye, the leader turned suddenly and they all followed, running down the hill in the opposite direction, away from us. I told Tracie and we both stopped for a moment, inhaled deeply and exhaled even deeper. Something had caught their attention. They had picked up on something emitting a frequency of fear and our love was no longer a match for them.

I felt elated; we looked at each other, sharing in the power and energy of the moment. We hugged each other tightly and laughed as we talked about the power of our thoughts. The aliveness and love we felt was out of this world. We both agreed there was not another person on Earth we would have wanted to go through this experience with other than each other, as both our life experiences had taught us how to respond to dangerous situations and our connection with the source of all creation was both strong and powerful.

On reaching the farmers' market our thoughts moved on to food, and we delighted in the fresh organic produce being offered to us. Fruit and vegetables, so many different colours and varieties, we were spoilt for choice. Some we'd never seen before, and we were eager to try out and experience all the new ones. The people were so nice and friendly and there always seemed to be someone around willing to step in to help with translation when needed.

We were so completely carried away with all the wonderful offerings and all the wonderful meals we were going to make, we didn't give the dogs a second thought and concentrated on stocking up. Armed with our supplies, both with bags in each hand, we headed back towards the dirt track. Everyone drove here and now we knew why. It was hard going, but it was a challenge we had been up for, well aware, before heading out, that it was all uphill on the way back. We had been busy chatting away when we heard the familiar barks in the distance and realised that we were coming up to the house where the dogs hung out. It's funny, because we both had the same thought, "What do I have in the bag to offer them if they do come?" Both of us spoke our thoughts at the same time. Tracie said, "bread," and I said, "fruit," and we laughed out loud at the idea of communicating telepathically. We knew we could and had done so on occasions, but mainly with looks rather than what just happened.

We stopped, put our bags down and took a breather. Even though we had managed to ward them off energetically last time, we both agreed we really didn't fancy doing it again and asked out loud for an angel and waited. Not a couple of minutes went by when a car appeared from around the bend. We were so happy to see it and thanked our creator out loud for responding so quickly. As the lady pulled up near us, we were so certain she was an angel sent just for us, we would have just opened the car doors and jumped in, thanking her with all our heart, but her car was a two-door, and, as she leant out of the window and spoke, we realised she only spoke Spanish. I only knew a few odd words, not enough to have a conversation, but it didn't really matter, she was our angel. We did excited hand gestures, thanking her for stopping, but she just looked at us, confused. She spoke so fast, it was hard to make out what she was saying, but the energy of her words were of concern and worry. The only word I heard that I knew was 'perro', meaning 'dog', so we said "Yes," nodding our heads in recognition, thinking she was now going to let us get in and take us safely up the mountain, but she shook her head, shrugged her shoulders and drove off.

Tracie and I looked at each other in disbelief. Did she not know she was our angel? Where was she going without us? Had she not felt the impulses of her spirit telling her to get us to safety?

It took us about five minutes to get over the shock but, when we did, we decided we had done it before so we could do it again. Consciously aligning ourselves with source, breathing in and out deeply and surrendering once again, we picked up the bags, ready to go. We hadn't taken one step forward before we heard a car behind us, coming just around the bend. We stopped and looked. It was Oliver's car. We laughed as he beeped and drove up to us. Clambering into the car, we told him he was our angel as we excitedly relayed what had happened. We told him about the dogs and our experience and the lady who we thought had been the angel we asked for. Oliver said he'd arrived home earlier than expected as his car miraculously got fixed quicker than anticipated. He'd returned to a worried Stacey and had set off again to look for us at the farmers' market and didn't know how we had managed to miss each other.

As we drove to the house, we realised we had been given, not one, but two angels. One was sent to delay us just long enough for the other one to reach us. On reflection that night, I thought it was so much better that way, to meet disappointment as the imposter it was, teaching us to keep our vibration on a higher level despite the circumstances and despite what reality looks like in any moment; expanding our perspective and creating much more of an experience.

I had known our visit to Costa was going to be a spiritual experience, but it really went beyond imagination. We are so much more than we think we are, and it sometimes takes extreme situations to bring you to that point where you have nowhere else to go but deeper within, further than you've ever been before and surrendering to release the essence of who you really are.

We had communicated telepathically that day, more than once, and I had incredibly translated the frequency the dog was sending out, hearing its words clearly. When we had first arrived, we had joked in the car on the way up about that same house being prepared for us, and I smiled, as it really had been, but not in the way we'd imagined.

Perro Reflections

This experience was all about frequency, mind over matter and changing matter with thoughts. It expanded me mentally, emotionally and spiritually, reinforcing my belief that by focusing all our attention on love we can send out a signal so high-pitched that any shade of darkness has no choice but to either move away, or be consumed and changed by it.

By putting obstacles in the path of the ants and observing their reaction, I realised they were so driven, so focused on their mission, they did not see the problem or an obstacle as something to overcome. It didn't stop them; they just kept their focus on the outcome they wanted and headed straight to it, creating new pathways for every new obstacle. It gave me clear insight to use this in my own life.

I realised that being in the jungle with wild animals and insects wasn't a fear for me and I happily slept with my window open, with only a piece of netting separating us, but at home, in England, no matter how hot it got, I would never sleep with my windows open. Humans appear to be much more of a danger to me than the wild animals of Costa Rica.

Food was the catalyst for this experience. The farmers' market was so near, yet so far away, tempting us with its offerings, but it was the hunger for adventure and excitement and new mystical experiences that had created it.

We spoke the experience into existence by our conversation about our vulnerability if a wild animal should come out of the jungle. It was our vibration of fear and the realisation there was nowhere and nothing much I could do that would set the stage for the new growth and over-standing.

The dogs appeared after sniffing out the frequency of fear we were giving out. The dogs' aggressive natures matched up and added to the already fearful thoughts swirling around in our minds, enhancing and further exaggerating the vibration of fear. You could say that our first thoughts were valid, and it's a reasonable thing to question what to do if a wild animal appeared. After all, the dogs may have been waiting there, anyway?

Or you could say that our vibration attracted them to us. After all, we were able to discontinue being a match for them once we changed our energy to Love.

When we first asked for help it was in panic and fear. I heard an audible voice saying he knows a way out. At first I wondered whether this voice had been something or someone else warning me, but the voice clearly said, "I know a way out." It was also the voice of something or someone in a heightened state of excitement. I believe, in my own conscious heightened state, I became a match to that same frequency and was able to translate the frequency to something audible.

It was when we changed our energy to one of pure love that we changed the outcome. Our words of help were more in line with appreciation and surrendering to the Higher Power and, in that surrendering, reclaimed our power. We then had the leverage of the universal forces all focused on our wellbeing.

Tracie and I had used telepathy before but when we both answered the question we had in our minds verbally at the same time, it made us know the connection we had was so much more than we ever truly realised. We have more power than we could ever use, and this has only enhanced my want and need to expand and unfold as I realise and begin to remember more and more of these powers.

The timing of both our angels was impeccable, divine timing, not stepping in a moment before it was necessary, making sure our experience was elongated, making sure we received and squeezed every last drop of insight out of our experience. One angel stopped, giving Oliver just enough time to rescue us, but it was only after we got over the shock of the lady driving off, stopped and re-centred ourselves again, ready to boldly head on in the direction of the dogs, that Oliver appeared round the bend. The levelling up and down we had to do in those precious moments worked our spiritual muscles to the max, creating and evolving us as spiritual beings.

It's funny how you joke about things and, on reflection, come to see them in a new, fresh light…we had said on our first day as we drove up that dirt track halfway up the mountain that the house being built was being prepared for us, and how very true those words were. As I pondered on this, the words 'home is where the heart is' came to mind, and I saw the significance between the house and our experience. Our heart is the energy centre that feels… it sends vibrations out into the universe, matching up and drawing to it things of the same vibration. The place we call 'Home' is somewhere we should feel safe, happy, a place of warmth and welcoming…. a place full of love. We are always at home when we keep the vibration of love alive, no matter what the situation is and no matter where we are.

This was an incredibly expanding experience and one that took me to a new level of understanding about vibrations and the power of our thoughts in any moment. It was incredibly difficult to sustain a level head and heart under these circumstances, but 'what is' in any moment changes with every moment and, instead of just seeing 'what is', we created the outcome we wanted instead of feeding what could possibly be, by staying rooted in fear. This takes me back to a time in Mexico where I rode the waves of upward and downward vibrations. Come with me, 'Downtown'…

Downtown

Unfortunately Lisa managed to get sunstroke on the first day at the beach. I had wanted her to let go a little but didn't mean not putting factor on. The mosquitoes loved her and she was hounded by them, each tiny mossie siphoning her blood through the tubes in their mouths and leaving behind a mound of infected saliva. Not only that, but she had somehow managed to get bitten by a spider, which was very painful and left behind a large swelling on her leg. If that wasn't enough, she had a mother of a cold sore on her mouth due to all the stress her body was under, her cells desperately trying to contain and heal the onslaught they were receiving all at once. I felt bad for the condition she was in, as Lisa worked hard at the hospital where she worked and really deserved this holiday.

We headed down to the reception to ask for a medic and, although the hotel was fully equipped with a doctor and medical necessities, Lisa needed antibiotics, creams and very strong painkillers, so the doctor wrote out a prescription for me to take to the pharmacy in town. As the doctor was giving me directions to the pharmacy, I was slightly distracted by the biggest lizard I've ever seen waddling out from behind a bush. At the same time, the doctor received a call to an incident that needed his expertise so was also distracted as he hurriedly pushed the paper into my hand and hurried off.

Lisa, feeling unwell, had gone to the room while I spoke to the doctor. She needed to lie down and was tucked up in bed, full up of painkillers, when I got to the room. Lisa offered to come with me, concerned about me going alone, but she was in no fit state, so I said no. Even though she was in a lot of pain she still tried to insist. I thought the idea was completely insane, so a small disagreement was had before I headed out, alone. I knew Lisa was only thinking of me but there were times when she really needed to think about herself. It was a beautiful, sunny morning, not a cloud in the sky, and I could feel it was going to be a hot one. As the automatic doors of the hotel opened, the aircon was exchanged for a warm breeze. The main road was about 50 metres away from the entrance of our hotel and, making one last check that I had all I needed, prescription, money, all there, I headed towards the bus stop.

The main road had a bus stop on either side, and I suddenly wondered which way I was heading. I tried to recall the conversation with the doctor and the instructions, but it was unclear. Oh! I would have to go back to reception to ask, I thought, but just then noticed a Mexican woman with two children waiting at the bus stop nearest to me and thought it would be quicker to ask her. As I reached her, she was chatting and laughing with her children who couldn't have been any older than 5 and 7, both becoming shy as I approached them. I noticed the light in their eyes as we exchanged smiles as I showed the woman my prescription. In broken English and hand gestures she explained, the other side of the road and the bus would be about 20 minutes. We exchanged smiles again as our eyes met and, thanking her, I crossed over to the other side.

At the other side was a ditch and a descending grassy area leading down to a river. The water was moving only very slightly as the leaf that had fallen into the water was barely moving. As I stood there, watching, I filled my lungs up, embracing the smell, the sight and the feel of Mexico. I was loving it here already. When I looked around again the woman and her children were disappearing onto the bus. I looked up the road for my bus. It would be easy to see as the road was long and straight and I'd always had really good long vision but, not seeing anything, I decided to take a closer look at the river. Carefully jumping over the ditch, I descended down the grassy slope to get a better look, but before I reached the bottom, I heard shouts. They sounded like someone warning someone of danger. I couldn't understand the words but the energy behind them was felt so I quickly scrambled back up to see what was happening.

I was met at the top by a small, elderly man. He seemed angry and was aiming it at me! He didn't speak English but gestured with his hands and I quickly began to realise he was warning me about the crocodiles that lived in the water. Defense mode kicked in. "Well, how was I to know! There are no warnings. Why is there no fence up? No notices?" The man gestured towards a small, unclear sign further along the road with a crocodile on it. How was I supposed to see that? My excited, happy vibration was now mixed with a frequency of fear and stupidity. After a few brief moments of being angry about the need for clear signs and fences, I decided to take responsibility for the incident. I was in an unfamiliar country and couldn't even speak their language. I should expect the unexpected. I knew this incident would not have happened in England where Health and Safety have gone mad, but this is Mexico.

The small man had replaced the woman and children at the bus stop opposite and, after a while I attempted to make light conversation in gestures with him, desperately trying to take his mind off what happened, as I was getting a little tired of seeing him shake his head from side to side in disbelief every time our eyes met. I told him I was going to the pharmacy and, from what I could make out, either bus will take you to one. I could see a bus coming down the road, far in the distance, but on the other side. My bus was nowhere in sight. It was starting to get really hot and there was no shelter on my side. I crossed the road just before the bus pulled up and spoke to the driver. In broken English he said there is a pharmacy downtown, at the last stop, but that it may be better if I wait for bus on other side. I quickly glanced around the bus; people were chatting and laughing. I felt for the energy and the vibe was good so I paid the fare and got on, hurrying past my rescuer who was thankfully looking out the window.

The bus was full and very lively, nothing like the busses back home where everyone pretends not to see you and peers distantly out of the window. I found a seat at the back and looked around. There was a good balance of male and female energies but I couldn't help noticing I was the only English (white) person on the bus. I chuckled to myself, we always do that don't we! We find someone, anyone like us, so we can feel comforted in what we think we know. We feel a little safer, a false sense of security, as if it makes a difference what nationality a person is. I laughed inwardly at my fear; I knew better. It's the energy and has nothing to do with appearances and, in the selecting of better thoughts, I started to relax. The driver was blaring out lively Mexican tunes really loudly, something that would never happen at home, and I loved the feeling of freedom it gave me. Someone started singing along to a tune and others joined in, slightly out of tune, but with such passion, and I was carried along with the vibration of fun, happiness and laughter. The windows were open and the cool breeze reached me far at the back along with a slight smell of food, body odour and body spray. The vibe was intoxicating, friendly and comforting and, despite not understanding a word, the energy made me feel really happy.

The bus got lighter as we travelled, making stops along the way, and people smiled and nodded to me as they left the bus. I had so wanted to see real Mexico, real people, not just the people working in the hotels, and I was feeling happy sitting in this bus and being a part of their lovely warmth. As I looked out of the window, I noticed the buildings begin to change. They were looking a little dirtier, the houses more rundown and an uneasy feeling started moving inside my stomach. I questioned my decision to board this bus and thought I should perhaps get off at the next stop and head back the other way, but it was overridden by a stronger one to see the journey through, regardless. After all, I only had to get Lisa's medication. How hard could it be?

The end of the road came, and I thanked the driver, who pointed to the stop I needed to get back. The town was not what I expected. It was definitely downtown, and not up. It didn't seem very busy either; I'd expected it to be bustling with activity. I passed some people sitting by the kerb, if you could call it that, as there didn't seem to be a beginning or an ending to the road, it just blended in. The people sitting there were drinking from a bottle as a couple of dogs, looking like a couple of square meals were in order, hunted for scraps close by. I didn't have any food on me, and I didn't want to stroke them as I might fall in love and want to take them home. There was nothing I could do but ignore them at all costs. It got a little busier, the further along I went, and I stuck out like a lighthouse in a storm as I felt the eyes of many on me… it's funny, the thoughts that come into your head sometimes, I remember my daughter Lydia's reply to me one day when I told her to put a coat on as she headed out of the house, "The eyes will keep me warm," she said, as she smiled and shut the door behind her. But the eyes were not keeping me warm, they were making me hot, and I was sweating. The looks seemed to say, "Why are you here? Are you mad?"

I stopped a woman, showing her my prescription, and she pointed in the direction of the pharmacy much further along. The uneasiness was creeping up inside me and getting stronger the further I went. I looked around for the bus stop the driver had told me about to get me back, and a wave of panic erupted in me as I did a 360 degree turn and could see nothing that I recognised - no landmarks, no bus stop, nothing. Men seemed to be appearing in doorways as I walked past. They were speaking in Spanish and laughing. I caught myself for a minute and asked myself if this was just my imagination or the tricks of my mind playing out the images, films and stuff accumulated throughout my years, bringing up emotions and fears of possibilities. I decided that, as I had been in some horrendous situations in the past, the danger was real. I also knew that I was a survivor, so I decided not to play the victim. Head up, chest out, exuding confidence is what's needed and, at that moment, I was very relieved to see the pharmacy.

Quickly hurrying inside, I patiently waited my turn. Luckily the list was in Spanish as nobody spoke English in the store. The people serving behind the counter looked surprised to see me and spoke together in Spanish whilst glancing at me, each look tightening the already anxious knot in my stomach as my mind made up thoughts of what they meant. As I left the store the sun beat down on the top of my head; no hat or shades. 'I must look like a crazy English woman,' I thought, squinting and sweating. I had managed to get a tan yesterday, but only on one side, and it was still a little on the pink side. My intention was to tan the other side today, once I got back. I was suddenly startled by a man sitting in a doorway next to the pharmacy. He looked up and said, "Ah Sonority, you gon' get kidnapped tonight." I think, for a few moments, my heart stopped beating before thumping back into action as I realised, I was holding my breath... how ironic, in a place where nobody speaks English, I managed to hear that loud and clear.

I recall breathing in deeply and out again, several times, as the knot was making my breathing shallow and my heartbeat faster, trying to cope with the lack of energy flow. I asked a passing woman for directions, but she hurried past, either not understanding me or too busy. I didn't know where to head. In panic mode, I headed along the high road, whispering, 'Am I going the right way? God help me!" A couple of minutes along the road, a Mexican man appeared at my side and spoke to me in fairly good English. He said he'd noticed me, and I looked lost. I joked, was it that obvious? I looked him straight in the eyes. I would know who he was by his eyes. They were a warm, deep brown and his soul shone through them, and I instantly felt safe and relaxed in his presence. He told me I was heading further downtown and didn't want to go there, and said he would escort me to the bus stop which would take me back to my hotel. He asked how I had managed to get myself down here, so I told my story from the beginning, explaining everything as we walked talked and laughed together. I told him about my desire to see real Mexico, real people and I had got my wish. He said, "Downtown is definitely real. The people are mostly good, they are kind and loving, and then there are the others, those that could make you disappear without a trace." He smiled at the look on my face and told me not to worry, the good weren't going to let that happen.

It took some time to reach our destination and I realised just how far I had walked. As we approached the stop, I told him what an angel he was and I thanked God for him. He smiled at the compliment as he held my hand in both hands and told me to take care. Before boarding the bus I hugged him with all the love I had inside me and kissed his cheek. My angel told me to keep embracing Mexico with an open mind and heart and Mexico will embrace you back. He spoke to the driver in Spanish, asking him to take special care of me and, as the bus pulled away, I looked at him through the window and put my hands over my heart in a gesture of the purest of love. I felt a surge of relief set in as I settled down into my seat, looking out of the window at my angel getting smaller and farther away, and I thanked God with all my heart.

"Wow, what an experience, what an adventure! Lisa will be shocked and a bit annoyed with me when I tell her," I thought, as I watched the buildings begin to change into hotels. I had wanted to see Mexico, not the touristy Mexico, and I had been given it. My journey had been full of ups and downs, feeling positive and feeling negative, my vibration attracting as I went. If I had got on the bus to uptown Mexico I would have missed out on this experience and the valuable feedback my inner light was showing me. It was not the situation I found myself in, but my thoughts about it that had impacted. The higher power, the divine energy force is always with me. I have freewill to choose my paths and I always seemed to choose the path that allowed for greater evolving of my soul.

I realised that day that I could ride the frequencies of life like I ride the bus, getting on and off with my thoughts. I knew I would always choose the bus that led to a more fulfilling ride and, even though, at times, the journey was dark and heavy, it would always be overtaken by the lightness and warmth of my angels.

Downtown reflections

I noticed how when someone is living on the hormones of stress, when that stress is taken away quickly, as in going on holiday and completely being stress-free, the body seems to get rid of it out of the body in some form of physical ailment.

From the beginning of my journey, it had all been about the thoughts I was having. I was lowering and raising my vibration with my thoughts about what was happening in any moment. Was the fear real? Or was it just a matter of the thoughts I had about it?

I had asked to see the real Mexico, and it didn't get much realer than that. Whenever I have an unexpected experience, I always look back to see if it was something I initiated and asked for. Then I look at where my thoughts and vibrations were as, most of the time, I can see the connection between the two.

After my incident with the river and the elderly man, my thoughts were to expect the unexpected, and the unexpected happened.

This experience was like a roller coaster ride of ups and downs and taught me a lot about where my thoughts were taking me. What was real? Were the threats real or were they in my mind? When we listen to our mind, we only have the experiences we have stored in our mind to guide us, but when we allow the bigger part of us to come forth, it uses our experiences as a means to unfold and emerge and to grow. I wondered where the fear had come from and where I had learnt it from. As long as I can remember, as a child, I was terrified of the dark, imagining all sorts of things, but was it a sensitivity to energies around, the streams of thought that were circling the airwaves? Had I tapped into the darker ones when night came, when I could no longer see the dancing particles? Yes, the dancing particles! This reminds me of an experience I had when I was young and, aptly named, let me take you to a story called 'Dancing'…

Dancing

As far back as I can remember I have loved dancing, even before my birth, while still being formed, I was dancing around inside my Mum's stomach and came out, into the world, dancing. I must have been picking up the vibes from the Jazz my Dad loved to play, the frequencies of 'It's a wonderful world' penetrating through the layers of Mum's skin, sending ripples of joy through me, along with an eagerness to discover for myself more about this wonderful world.

I grew up in a home full of the sounds of Jazz, Blues and Opera. I had been born a few years before the birth of Beetle mania. Tunes such as 'Love me do' and 'I wanna hold your hand' were played constantly through the air waves. It was also around the time Martin Luther King delivered, with his beautiful energy, those famous words, 'I HAD A DREAM', and, whenever I heard those words, something inside me came alive.

When I was around 3 years old, we were on a shopping trip to one of the large department stores. One of the podiums where the mannequins stood was empty whilst the assistant clothed and prepared it nearby. Music was being piped through the store as I skipped along, listening to it, when one of my favourite tunes came flooding through. It was Freddie and the Dreamers, 'You were made for me'. The podium must have looked like a stage to me, and I slipped my hand out of my sister's and ran to my stage to dance. There I became encapsulated, completely taken over by the music, me and the frequencies, in a world of our own. I only became conscious of the crowd that had gathered, delighted by the spectacle of such a tiny person fully engrossed in the music, when the song ended, and I was rudely awakened from my state of being by the clapping and cheering.

It's only now I realised that my Mum had the patience of a saint. I would ask her to watch me dance. "Watch me be a tree," I'd say, and she would stop what she was doing to watch patiently while I gently danced in the breeze, then my arms going everywhere as the wind got stronger and stepping up the pace to a full-blown hurricane. As I grew, Mum was fully aware of my love of movement and asked me one day if I'd like to take a dance class. Penny Club was offering ballet, tap and ballroom for a penny a class and I excitedly said 'yes' to all three. I loved the way dancers moved in harmony, gliding and working together. I appreciated the way they flowed, as if their minds had left them, allowing their bodies the freedom to speak. I noticed how some dancers seemed to have that special 'something'. There was always that dancer, although doing the same moves, the same routine, they just stood out and shined. Was it learnt? Did it come from somewhere inside? Or was it from somewhere else?

I tried each class but, with each one, I quickly lost interest. I got bored of copying the steps. I could copy them to some degree, but then my feet would start rebelling, the energy in my body taking me in the opposite direction than what I was supposed to do. The music moved me in a different way, and I resonated with Frank Sinatra's song, 'I won't Dance', with the line, 'My heart won't let my feet do things that they should do'. It all came to a head during my tap-dancing class. I had been told to copy the steps a certain way several times, without success, and the teacher began to lose patience with me; I felt the irritation in her voice and the impatience in her tone as she abruptly asked me to do it again. I wasn't a rude child. My parents had taught me to be polite, but I realised it wasn't working the teacher's way, so, in my innocence, I suggested she try it my way and I showed her my moves. She was not amused, and I was told to either behave or get out, so I got out.

I am not sure when I started seeing the tiny golden particles that danced in the sky, but I must have been very young, as I don't recall ever not seeing them. Anytime I looked up in the sky, no matter what the weather, they were always there, shining and dancing like little sparks of pure energy. I found them beautiful and comforting, and they somehow felt like a part of me, but how could that be when I was here and they were way up in the sky, yet, somehow we communicated energetically. I always needed to be outside. I wanted to run, climb, dance, move and create, to express myself in my own way. The golden particles seemed to encourage me to play, as if in harmony with my own energy. Some days there even seemed to be a pulse behind them, as if the sky had a heartbeat of its own.

I had spoken about them briefly to my friends, expecting them to know what I was talking about, but nobody seemed to see them and started to make fun of me, so I stopped mentioning them and just enjoyed them. One rainy day I was pacing up and down the living room, looking out the window every now and again at the puddles and trying to convince my parents that the rain was stopping. My younger sister and brother were happily engrossed in the white Lego bricks that always came out from underneath the sofa whenever there was a need for construction. Mum was rattling around in the kitchen as another cup of tea was being made, and Dad sat reading his newspaper. Looking out of the window, it appeared to be slowing down a little, or so I imagined, so I asked Dad once again if I could go out. Not even raising his eyes, Dad spoke in a tone I was all too familiar with when he started to lose patience and said, "NO, it's raining." I knew I was in the process of losing this battle so, with nothing left to lose, I said, "Dad, the golden lights want me too.". That got his attention; he put his newspaper down in his lap and asked me, "What golden lights?" And, as I told him about them, I saw the light in his eyes brighten. He was looking at me, but through me at the same time. It took him ages to speak, but when he did, he smiled and told me I could go out. Dad understood something, that there was a deeper meaning behind it all, but this wasn't the time for me to know or question anything and I left the house in a hurry, just in case he changed his mind.

I left school at 15 without taking my exams. I had discussed it with my parents, and they agreed, as long as I found myself a job. They had never pushed me with school or homework but did say it may be harder for me to get a job if I decided not to take them. I felt like I had learnt all the necessary things, English, math, reading and writing, but felt I hadn't retained any other information. I much preferred sitting by the window, daydreaming, or just observing others around me. Despite studying for two years, I can still only remember a few words of French: 'tableau', 'un chien' and 'un chat', table, a dog and a cat. I couldn't see how that would help in any chosen career. It's funny how I excelled in some lessons, despite not liking the subject. It was all about the teacher and how they taught. If they made it interesting and engaging, I absorbed the energy from it, but when the teacher left and was replaced by another, I quickly lost interest as the subject became boring again.

Before leaving school, the careers advisor asked me what I wanted to do. I said 'dance'. She asked me what lessons I'd taken and what level I was at and, as I explained the situation, she looked at me over the top of her glasses and chuckled, explaining all the reasons why it wouldn't work and earn me any money. I was told that to be any good at dance I should have started when I was young. I didn't even know what style of dancing I wanted to do, and I couldn't even teach because I wasn't trained myself. The careers officer advised me to seek work in an office, otherwise I would be unable to earn a living. I knew she was advising me the best she could, and I did see her point but, as I closed the door behind me, I felt truly deflated. I felt like I had just landed badly after the most amazing parachute jump from a great height where the view from my higher perspective had been breath-taking. The wind, no longer keeping me uplifted, had left dropping me heavily on the ground.

That faithful knot in my stomach returned as I thought about office work. Oh God, I would be confined again, and the knot tightened as a wave of dread rose up, threatening to overspill from my eyes. As I walked along the corridor, blinking wildly, trying to push the tears back into my body, a familiar voice came drifting towards me. It was coming from one of the classrooms. Martin Luther King came flowing through the cracks in the door as I walked past, just at the right time. "I HAD A DREAM!", was all I heard. It was all I needed. Mr King had come to raise me up again. I felt the power and energy in his words and the uplifting of my soul and knew, in that moment, SO DID I! I wanted so much, not just for myself, but for everyone. I saw injustice, I felt the pain, and I wanted the world to change. My dreams, like seeds, had been planted deep within me, just waiting for the ideal conditions for the upward journey. The roots would find a foothold, growing strong in the darkness, all the time being fed and watered by life. I knew the foundation, once established, would allow the releasing of the divine ideas inside, where they would travel in a constant seeking of light, until finally bursting through to reveal the full fruition of the beautiful expressions inside.

As the energy came flooding back into me, I felt the up-draught raising me higher and higher. I realised the wind had not left me for good, had not left me on the ground, twisted and broken. It had gone for the King to raise my spirit again. I was being assisted and guided, but I had to know deep down in my soul that it was the thoughts and feelings I chose to focus on that held the power. I could have all the help I needed, but had to have the eyes to see it clearly, that only I have the real power to pick myself up and put my feet safely back on the ground.

Dancing reflections

I realised what an impact words have on us as children, each one having the power to affect or infect us, and this is highlighted and exaggerated by the energy in which the words are spoken.

Music is powerful and the frequencies put out by music plays and dances with our internal vibrations, having a profound effect on us.

As a child, I would go so completely into a world of my own when immersed in music. Some would call it 'the zone', where the outer world does not exist anymore and the only 'real' thing is the feeling of the flow and the connection to something much bigger.

I could copy the steps of a dance to some degree, as we all can, but found it boring learning someone else's dance. I wanted to create, to move in my own way, feel the music the way I did, and not how someone else did.

I should have been advised to follow my dreams, no matter what, even if I didn't know what my dreams were and I could earn a living by working in an office until I figured it out. not give up on them because they can't be done. Dreams should be embraced as a gift and not forgotten.

We are all born with gifts and talents and seeds of the dreams we have to birth into the world. There are those so caught up in the framework of so-called 'life', that they die with their seeds still unopened.

How beautiful that the powerful words I heard as a young child came back to assist me just at the right time…the energy, the spirit is always working. We just have to open ourselves up to hear it.

I know the words of Mr King were greatly felt by many and from all walks of life and nationalities. His words reached in, inspiring hearts, not just at the time, but for many years after. I realised how powerful words were and how they impacted us, especially the intention and energy behind them. Words mixed with the right frequencies of music could penetrate through the layers of your skin and dance in tune with your own soul's song. When my granddaughter was born, I realised that babies are so in tune with these frequencies and are so susceptible to the vibration of them, so I'd really like to take you to a memory called 'Kyiane'…

Kyiane

She emerged into the world on the 4th of July, American Independence Day. A tiny bundle of pure light, weighing only 4lbs, she was the tiniest being I'd ever seen, touched or held, and she immediately brought out feelings of protection and love. Her tiny hand wrapped tightly around my finger, exaggerating the smallness of her form. This little being was tiny, yes, but weak, no! She made her presence known and her lungs and voice bellowed out when she wanted to express what she was feeling. The sound and strength she made was so funny, as it didn't match her size. All who saw her, melted, as this tiny vision looked straight at you as soon as you talked to her, and she was alert and listening, picking up your every word. My home life at that time was still dysfunctional, but my thoughts about her were that I had so much to teach this little one.

Ky was only a few weeks old, but she seemed to cry much more than other babies. She would be sound asleep on your chest while you watched TV, snuggled up together, but it wouldn't take long before the chin would start to waiver and she would start to cry. The cry was heartfelt and would come from somewhere deep inside her. She didn't need anything, she had been fed, winded, bathed, changed and played with, but every now and again she would just start to cry for no apparent reason. Her Mum Maxine started to think something was wrong with her; she was definitely bothered by something, so Max had her checked over by the doctors. Max was told she had colic but, despite that, she was in perfect health.

Max tried to pacify her, but she was like a runaway train once she started and, once she gained momentum, it was hard to stop her. Max lived just around the corner from me and one day she came round in tears. Ky wouldn't stop crying. Max was so tired and at her wits end and desperate for some peace. I took Ky in my arms and told Max to make a cup of tea. I took the crying little bundle into the living room. The TV was on and I took her blanket off her and held her close to my chest. Our hearts were level with each other, mine was calm and hers beating twice as fast through all the crying. I walked round the room, talking softly, and she continued crying as I rocked her up and down in my arms. A tune came on the TV, and I could see her eyes look in the direction of where the sound was coming from; she stopped crying for a minute and appeared to be listening, so I continued to rock her and began singing along with the tune. Looking down at her, I could see she was intently listening, so I began to dance to the tune, keeping her close to me. After a while Max crept quietly into the room, asking if she had fallen asleep, but her eyes were wide open, alert and listening to the music.

As the tune ended, she began to turn her head, trying to pick it up again, but when she realised it was no longer there, the quiver in her bottom lip reappeared. I told Max to put on my player. Hip hop was on the tape and as it played the quiver subsided and she lay there looking at me and listening as I sang along. Ky had her hand completely wrapped around my finger and she held on tightly with such strength. I started to dance and felt our heartbeats beating as one as we danced both in sync with the frequencies of the music and, after a short while, she fell peacefully to sleep.

Max brought her round to me quite often after that. She would come around after a bout of crying and ask me to do the Hip Hop dance, as we called it. We thought it was funny that, despite her being so very young, she responded to the music the way she did. Soon after this realisation I started to observe her very closely and experimented with different genres of music. When I played slow jams or love songs her chin would quiver and she would begin to cry, and that heart-felt cry would rise up from a place deep within her. As soon as I changed it to something livelier, some house or soul, she would stop. I realised that, although she suffered with colic, it was the songs on TV that were causing her to cry, the music she was hearing, the adverts, the films, the peoples' voices. She was picking up the frequencies and translating them into feelings.

That's when I began to really realise the power of the frequencies and vibrations that get sent out. This little bundle of light was able to show me. She was pure light energy, born into a world full of frequencies. She picked up each frequency, translating the emotions through them and, because her heart was so open, they caused feelings inside her that made her either happy or sad.

Ky was only a few weeks' old and we already had a strong connection. She knew I loved her; she could feel it. She knew straight away if whoever was holding her was calm, as she was at peace in their arms. I had to prepare myself emotionally for when I picked her up and held her to me, as I knew she would know instantly if my feelings were anything other than peaceful. Most of us are unaware that we are sending out and picking up these frequencies every moment of every day, but Ky made me realise how powerful they were. I'd never met a baby like Ky before, so newly born and so in tune with the universe, one that would cry at the singing in an advert if it had any frequency of sadness in it.

As she grew, music became a major part in her life; she was always singing and dancing. The depth of feeling she had in her voice when she sang connected with something deep inside you, giving you goose bumps and bringing you to tears. It was the same for anyone listening. It was something pure, it was divine, and it was a gift to the world that she was born being able to translate the emotional frequencies without first learning them and being conscious of them. This tiny baby made me realise that my life experiences had made me emotionally desensitised and cut off from the frequencies of others. I had closed myself off and was operating in survival mode, and I had to open myself up to my true essence and allow my feelings to surface.

They say words don't teach, and this little baby couldn't speak, but as I held her in my arms and she held on tightly to my finger, our hearts beating as one, she helped me to remember to open my heart again. No matter what challenges life throws at us, we need to keep our hearts open to feel the frequencies of life and, in following our good feelings, this is how we make the choices that lead us towards our happiness. This tiny baby that I felt I had years of experiences to teach had, in only a few short weeks of being on this planet now, become my teacher.

Kyiane reflections

I had known the power of music before this, as I had been touched by music all my life, but I was now aware of just how powerful it was. We are flitting in and out of frequencies all day, every moment of the day, most of the time unconsciously, and are either being affected positively or infected negatively in each moment.

When I was a teenager, my Dad would tell me my eyes, along with my attitude, changed when I would come downstairs after a session of listening to certain music in my room. I took no notice of him at that stage as I was rebelling against being told anything, but now I know how the frequencies of certain music can and do affect your physical, mental and spiritual body.

I realised how susceptible babies are to these frequencies, being pure beings of light with no resistance, they just absorb it through their senses. We have to be conscious of what we are putting into them through music, energy and our words.

This was a great learning curve for me, and she came along at the right time to help me to understand how powerful the energy of everything is and, especially how it affects the little ones coming in. It made me laugh, how I thought I had so much to teach her and, of course I did, but it wasn't about that. The little ones are here to teach us and we have to be open to learn from them. This really does flow into an experience I had where I visualised the frequencies, really understanding them in a new way. This experience is called 'Rooftop'…

Rooftop

We had an event coming up in the next couple of weeks and the radio station was a hive of activity, with DJ's and MC's plugging it on every show. Competitions were being held and the airwaves were saturated with information, focused on getting as much attention and hype around our event as possible. It fascinated me, how, from a small room somewhere in North London, on a good day and with a good rig, the sound waves could travel as far out as Kent. I was very aware of the importance of everything that was said and done over the radio; there were vast amounts of people listening, some interacting and many other silent listeners. Many youngsters looked up to the DJ's and MC's and were influenced by their output, aspiring to one day be like them, having a show on the station and playing out at events. The radio was a life saver for many youngsters, giving them hope of a way out of their sometimes-troubled environments and lifestyles.

D.T.I., as they were known back then, was always listening, trying to track us to take us off the air. We had a good relationship with them. We understood they had a job to do, and there was a kind of understanding between us. We didn't see them as the enemy. It was a situation where they were just doing their job and we would often dedicate a tune or send a shout-out to them, especially on those cold, dark nights when we knew they were driving around at all hours of the night in their vans with the big antennas on the top. We kept in line with what we thought was right, didn't permit bad language on the radio and kept to a watershed. Certain things were not being played until after 9pm.

When they took our rig, they would normally take off the other stations at the same time, having tracked us all. There would be a raid and we would all be taken off air. Then we would need to get another rig and aerial put up on another building as quickly as possible. One night, after we were taken off, Maurice went up on the roof to see what could be salvaged and found a note apologising for having to take us off air. It was a nice gesture, and appreciated, and was confirmation of the respectful relationship we had built up. Maurice had started the station many years ago and was established when my eldest daughter met him. She soon became a big influence in the station becoming more, and then, together, they went on to win the UK Garage Awards. The constant battle of wills between them as to how the station should run soon took its toll, and the passion that was once alive, died down to a slight simmer. The station had been through many ups and downs along the way, along with many name changes, before I came along. The fire had gone out and the station, just barely running, was sometimes off air for weeks at a time and, at this point Maurice was considering selling it. I saw its potential and felt enthusiastic about breathing life into it again and stoking that fire. I had a fresh pair of eyes to see what needed to change and knew I could ignite that fire again and keep it burning. I wanted complete freedom to make the changes that needed to take place so. after many conversations and discussions. it was agreed that Maurice would look after the technical side of things. and I would run and manage the station with the understanding that any changes I wanted to implement would be run by Maurice and Max first.

I loved the fact that the station gave the DJ's MC's, singers and songwriters a real chance to showcase their talents. Many had come through the station to go on to making it big on the music scene. I saw it as having a foot in the door to the music industry, allowing some of the talented kids from the streets to slide through. We gave them a platform to learn their craft and finely tune the art of mixing, learning to connect with their audience in their own way, to find their own unique styles so they could expand and grow, bringing more of their individual personality to life. I knew how powerful words and music were and the effect it had on those people listening in, and knew the impact it had on the listeners, both young and old, and wanted our station to set the example for those aspiring to be on it. Our people were given complete freedom of expression, as long as there was no bad language or airing of grievances over the airwaves, either directly or indirectly. There were other stations to go to if they wanted that. Our DJ's and MC's knew one of us was always listening in to the shows. I had an earpiece in one of my ears at all times, unless I was sleeping, much to the annoyance of family and friends. I would ring up the show if I heard anything I didn't like, and also to congratulate them when they sounded really good.

Maurice sorted out the technical issues and was really good at always making sure we sounded crisp and clear and were not bleeding into any other radio stations. We had started buying better quality rigs and they were very powerful and had to be tuned just so. We even got to the stage where we had a few put aside for when we were taken off so we could go straight back on again in another location. I loved the way Maurice had learnt how to set it all up by himself. He hadn't learnt it at school or college; just fiddled around and worked things out 'til he had a clear understanding of how it all worked. It had all started when he was a young boy in Jamaica and had received a gift of a radio from his Dad. He was fascinated by the voices and music that came out of it and wondered how they got there. With his desire growing, he took it apart, opening it up to see all the co-operative components and elements inside. He had dismantled the radio, bit by bit, to gain a clear understanding of how it worked and then attempted to put it back together again. This was the start of his love affair with the waves that surfed the air.

One night I received a call from Maurice. The station had gone off air. He knew by the sound coming out of the radio that the rig was still in, so he knew it wasn't D.T.I.. By the sound coming out of the radio he could tell it was the aerial that had come loose. The aerial had to be put up as high as possible to give out the best signal. With no obstruction in its way the signals were much clearer. On this particular night, the wind was blowing so hard it had been forced away from the frame. Usually there were more than enough DJ's to help Maurice on the roof, but on this particular windy night nobody was available so he rang me to let me know he would sort it in the morning. We had a big event coming up and needed the station on to raise as much awareness as possible about it. Even if we didn't have DJ's playing live, we would have our music CDs playing all pre-recorded with our ads and upcoming events on for all our late-night listeners.

I suggested that I could hold a ladder, if that's all that needed to be done. At first it was just a passing thought, but I was suddenly excited at the prospect of being on the roof and pushed the point across. Maurice declined as it was far too dangerous but, after a short discussion about our upcoming event and the DJ's expected early in the morning, he decided it was worth driving over to get me. High up on the roof I began to see his point. There were no safety rails and the wind was blowing fiercely. We looked up at the aerial being thrown around as the wind howled around us and Maurice said this was way too dangerous. I agreed and suggested coming back in the early hours. We looked at each other, then the aerial, and then Maurice decided that, as we were already here, he may as well go ahead and get the job done.

I held the ladder tightly, positioning my feet and all of my body towards keeping the ladder stable as Maurice climbed up, trying to hold on for dear life. One hand gripped on the rung of the ladder as he desperately tried to grab the swinging aerial with the other. The wind was getting stronger the higher he climbed and seemed to almost enjoy trying to knock him off as he attempted to wrap the aerial tightly with the tape. It seemed to take ages and, by the time he had managed to secure it, my hands and body were frozen and blue, not with the cold but the intensity of holding the ladder restricting my blood flow. The wind may have been having its fun but all I knew was this ladder would not move, not on my watch.

After many attempts it was finally secured. Maurice, relieved to be on firmer ground, needed to sit down for a minute and I welcomed it, so we sat with our backs up against a tank of some sort. We sat there for ages, in silence, just looking out at all the lights, listening to the howling wind and observing until Maurice broke the silence. He said, "Do you know, if we had infrared goggles we would be able to see millions of frequencies passing through each other, signals being sent out across the sky?" I sat there, pondering the thought and imagined seeing them littering the night sky. I saw them passing through me as I sat there; they were all different sizes, strengths and even colours. I visualised how far they travelled and the many people they reached and passed through. I realised how this affects the energy in our bodies as we unconsciously move through one to the other during the day, completely unaware of the many moving sound and light frequencies moving through us in every moment.

Whilst I sat there, I saw the importance of the station and what it really was. I saw the real value in that moment. I thought about the event we had coming up and how most of the DJ's were unaware of the important role they played. They were supposed to be taking you on a journey; it should be a continuous upward flow, each tune raising your vibration and energy that little bit more. Each DJ in sync with each other, raising the stakes with precisely executed tunes, taking you higher and higher into a heightened state of bliss. I was finding that it was rarely like that, no matter what event we put on or where I went, there seemed to be DJ's playing to themselves, seemingly unaware that people had stopped dancing. There were those tunes I called drink-or-toilet tunes because, after playing a few uplifting ones, they would drop a tune that quickly deflated the energy and vibe so I would use this time to get myself a drink, speak to people or use the loo. A great DJ would have me there, wanting to go to the toilet but not wanting to miss out on the feeling being evoked in me. There were those DJ's so in sync with the tune they were playing, they added elements of themselves, pieces of their souls, that were felt by everyone. These were special DJ's. They played with their spirit at the decks, completely and utterly not lost but found in the moment. The crowd knew it; it was a vibe that called you to the dance floor. It was not just about the music it was about how the music made you feel. It was about the frequencies and how they played and danced with your internal energy. I had played with frequencies all my life; I grew up in a house filled with blues, jazz and opera. As a young child I felt the raising of my spirit when certain tunes were played, and the lowering as I felt the sadness in others. Some tunes had no words, but each one was speaking in a language I could hear, feel and understand. I would cry as the instruments spoke to each other, relaying stories of loss and loneliness, and would dance around the living room in pure joy as they found their connection to their power again.

It was whilst I was in this place that I realised no matter what DJ was playing, there was not a continuous elevation in the tunes being played. You would be taken so far and then the next tune played would bring you down a level and not up. There needed to be a continual flow of uplifting energy but, in truth, it was staggered up and down. Don't get me wrong, most of the tunes being played fitted together and were mostly mixed to perfection, but they didn't take you on a journey of uplifting vibrations. I was sitting there, taking it all in, when Maurice started chatting again. I glanced at him, his mouth was moving, but I couldn't hear his words. The satisfaction of the thoughts I was receiving was blocking him out. All of a sudden, I received a thought about getting each main radio station from all corners of London, N.E.S.W, together in collaboration, bringing London together in a frequency of Love and Peace. I could see it; I felt it and knew it could happen. Music and dance were the elements, and it was all about frequencies. We don't just hear the words and music, we feel them. That's why Music is so powerful. With the right music and the right words, you have the perfect combination of inspiration and vibration.

Earlier on in my life, many years before I became a part of the station, I had received a dream about having an event in a castle with a large moat around it. The dream had been so vivid and real and, I not only saw it very clearly but, I had powerfully felt it. Not seeing its relevance at the time, it was allowed to sit quietly at the back of my mind but, all of a sudden, it came back full force... My dream was a vision, it was something to be created, and it was something completely different, something new and exciting. I could see it so clearly. We would have all the elements of music that healed you from the inside.

Not just MC's but Inspirational speakers, inspiring and uplifting, taking you to new heights with the energy of their words. There would be meaningful films, healthy food and nourishment, places to rest and sleep. Everything you could want or need would be in the castle. You would be invited to come for the weekend and, once the drawbridge was raised, you stayed for the journey, the journey you'd take inside yourself, raising your awareness, your consciousness, your vibration and energy alongside others.

First, there was much to do. I had to implement the changes at the station. It wouldn't be easy. I didn't own the station, I managed it, and had already come across power struggles. Being female in a male-dominated environment meant we had very different ways of looking at things. I had found, despite wanting to improve things, that there were ingrained ways of doing things and change didn't come easily, even if it was for the better. I also had to get them to understand about the frequencies they were giving out and try to implement change in the way we played, and what we played. Once we got that right, why stop at London, why not go to all four corners of England, and then the world?

I was in my element and felt so satisfied, sitting there, receiving more and more downloads and playing with all the thoughts that were coming to me. The idea of bringing all four corners together, N.E.S.W, in a collaboration raising people up with our music, taking them on a journey, raising and uplifting them through frequency and vibration, started to make complete sense and tied in with what I was receiving loud and clear, and I laughed out loud as I suddenly realised the relevance of my dream and why the event had been in a castle…because a castle has wings!

Rooftop reflections

This experience was one of those defining moments when all the pieces start to fit together like a big life puzzle. About six months after this I met the most amazing woman who had a vision similar to mine. Tracie had already attempted creating and bringing a similar vision to life, but the components weren't co-operative. We both had some more growing to do before this could come together in its fullness and entirety and, as always, in divine timing.

The radio station really was a lifesaver for some; it gave the young people a release from the pressures they were facing. Some only needed it for a while until they found other things to amuse themselves with, but others went on to make a career out of their pastime. I wonder how many think back to their times on the radio and reflect on how it assisted in their growth.

The relationship with D.T.I. showed me that, although you may be on opposing sides with someone, if you don't take things personally and always connect with the bigger part of them, even in the division you can still create a good relationship and a sense of unity. It's all about your thoughts and perceptions.

I saw how power struggles can be so destructive to what is being created. When we come together as a team, without the egos, we can build and create something beautiful. I have found that a great team consists of people who can see the vision and will assist in its creation because it should be created, not because of what they can get out of it.

My desire to get to the station on that night, and the sudden interest in going onto the roof, allowed me to experience the next stage of the dream. My inner being guided me to the next step in its evolution.

Sometimes vivid dreams are visions and, as you continue your journey through life, all the different elements start coming together for it all to flow to you in a way that is delightful and unexpected.

My time with the radio station was amazing, I learnt so much, especially about frequencies. Having to organise and manage young males, some with especially large egos, was sometimes challenging but very rewarding. I loved seeing them progress and, once they accepted that everything I was doing was for the good of the station, they started to understand me. This was also a healing time for me; I had been re-housed after being in a womens' refuge, so was eager and excited for this next phase in my journey. I was releasing old patterns of thinking and behaviour and returning to a self that I was familiar with. I was remembering my gifts and talents and coming to a new understanding that there was much more to me than I thought. I would like to take you to a healing experience I had that was to change my perception forever. Come with me now to 'Songbird'…

Songbird

I t was the middle of Spring; the leaves on the trees were out in full force, making a safe place for the flowers to make their entrance into the world. Only a few weeks ago they had looked so bare and lifeless, the beauty of their existence completely hidden from view, but it was all just sitting there waiting for the right time, the perfect moment to bloom and unfold. The flowers were now just bursting to open up, to reveal the perfection of their colour, texture and fragrance; everything was emerging, expanding and coming alive. This time of year had come to be very special to me and, looking back, it had always been a time of rebirth and renewal.

This particular morning, I had woken up with an air of excited expectancy. You know, that kind of morning where you can't quite put your finger on it but you just know today is going to be a good day. My daughter, Lydia, all grown up with a son of her own, was due to have a therapy session for her childhood trauma. A psychologist friend of mine had created a new system. He had been inspired to create a unique way of assisting and empowering people and Garvey would be seeing my daughter this morning. I hadn't known him long but, from the moment I met him, I instinctively trusted him. He had a good heart and I knew he had received his system from a good place.

Although feeling very anxious, my daughter was exhausted from the heavy weight she carried around with her and was tired of picking the scabs from her internal sores, making them bleed. For the session they were using an office which was in a courtyard just opposite my flat on the 1st floor. The courtyard was surrounded by flats and was always quite busy, with people coming and going, but it had a grassy area filled with plants and one big old tree which had been there for years.

After seeing them into the office and closing the door I intended to go home to clean and potter about my house but, as I walked away I noticed a young bird. It looked like a baby Song Thrush; it was fluffy brown with faint speckles on its chest and it was clinging onto a fence and flapping desperately. I could see feathers everywhere, mixed with spots of blood. Then I noticed the cat; it was black and white with feathers stuck to its mouth. My heart began to race and I knew I had to act quickly, so I started clapping my hands to shoo the cat away. As the cat reluctantly skulked away it looked back once to give me a look of pure annoyance for stopping its little bit of fun, before disappearing into a garden.

I tried to grab hold of the bird, but it was panicking. I wouldn't leave it there, injured. The cat would definitely come back. I had always rescued injured birds as a child, bringing them to my Dad and, together, we would make a bed for them in a box on our balcony. Sometimes all they needed was a safe place to rest and, other times just a safe place to die. I tried again to get a firm grip on the baby bird who was now terrified, fighting for her life and was desperately trying to get away from me. After several failed attempts I spoke aloud, "Oh please help me!" and, the next moment, I managed to get a firm hold. As I held her, I could feel her blood between my fingers and her little heart beating so fast, I thought that she would die of shock. She hadn't been long on this Earth and her first attempt at flying and becoming independent had her mauled by a cat and now, to make matters worse, a dreaded human had her in a grip. Her survival instincts were kicking in, telling her this was a dangerous position to be in.

My daughter wasn't due out for an hour and, although they probably hadn't started yet, I thought there was no way I was going to interrupt. I looked around for somebody, anybody, but no-one appeared. I had the keys to my flat in my bag which was slung over my shoulder and both my hands were busy. My thoughts were to get into my house, clean her up and assess the damage, but that did not look like it was happening. I looked around again for somebody to help but saw no-one, and I thought, "Why isn't there anyone around when you need them?" I walked up to the first-floor landing and stood outside my front door, both me and the baby bird feeling helpless and anxious. "Now what?", I thought, as I stood overlooking the courtyard watching the feathers brutally torn from her fluffy soft chest dancing freely, without a care in the world in the breeze. I realised I could do nothing, so I perched my arms on the bar for some relief. Being completely in that moment I could feel the bird's heartbeat still beating fast and realised it matched my own. Suddenly conscious, I started breathing deeply, as I had done many times before, calming my heart rate right down and, as I did, so the bird's heartbeat began to slow down too. I spoke to her in a soft, reassuring tone, telling her it was ok, she was safe, and she seemed to be listening. I started to think that she was hurt pretty badly and if she died, at least I will have given her a safe place to die peacefully. It was the most I could do. Then, in a flash, I caught myself. What was I thinking? I thought of my daughter in therapy; yes, she's hurt but it's far from over. I remembered the power of healing; I remembered everything is energy. This baby bird was in my hands and my thoughts and feelings have power; she will live! "Help me," I whispered.

Focusing intently on my heartbeat, then on hers, I saw them beating as one. I focused on the crown of my head opening up, the once soft spot we have as babies, our divine connection to the higher power before it hardens as we learn and grow. As I allowed my crown to open, I felt the stream of liquid love from the source of all creation flowing through me, flooding my whole body with light. I felt the flow travelling through my body and felt the connection as it reached my hands, flooding this precious little spirit with love and wellness. I visualised her singing every morning, just before the sun rose, in appreciation of the new day ahead, and watched as she soared above the trees, looking down on Earth from her bird's eye view of the world. I didn't hope. I didn't believe. I knew she would live.

I am not sure how long I was there in the zone, but it must have been at least 30 minutes. Time didn't exist. There was no time in this place of no matter. There was just space, and we were completely embraced in light. During this time nobody passed, nobody was seen in the courtyard, and I don't even recall seeing or hearing any birds. Maybe I was so caught up, I hadn't noticed. I felt the surrender of the baby to the energy as it felt the love from its creator through me and a vibration of peacefulness and calm wrapped its arms around us, engulfing us both. After a time, I slowly became aware of my surroundings again. The blood that had felt moist between my fingers had dried up, and I knew I would be guided when the time came for the next step. I'd receive an impulse, and I just had to remain in the moment. From the rooftop just to my right, perched on an antenna, a bird appeared. It called out and my baby turned its head from side to side, trying to receive the signal clearer, just like you would tune your radio. The calls began getting louder and more frequent, and my baby's eyes started to sparkle with every call. The mother was calling her baby to her.

I spoke to her, telling her all was well, "Mummy's here now". She looked around at me and closed her eyelids once before giving her body a little wiggle, letting me know she was ready and, on the next call, I opened my hands, and she flew effortlessly to the rooftop. I watched them talking back and forth until, finally, Mum flew to her. I cannot express in words the feeling I felt as the words have not been created to describe it, and I don't think they ever will be as the feeling was not of this world. In that moment I felt completely and utterly connected to every living thing on this planet, and beyond. I am still in awe and live in appreciation of the beautiful experience created and so thankful I chose to take the opportunity in allowing the power to take over.

My daughter continues to go from strength to strength. She has her battle scars, but they no longer bleed. She has felt the power of source energy and knows it's constantly flowing to her, and she continues to open herself up to receive it. The Song Thrush brings a message from the spiritual realms of survival and basic needs in life, home, family and people around us that care. Sometimes, during my early morning meditation, I hear a bird singing sweetly at the top of its voice and I can hear and feel the vibration of love in its song. I know it's her, once again in harmony with me, together appreciating this new day.

Songbird reflections

This was a beautiful experience of surrender. It shows the power of letting go, getting out of the way to allow the flow of pure love energy to fully take over. We all have this ability, but we have forgotten, as we focus our attention on the things of this world that hurt us, rather than heal.

The baby bird was so frightened that I couldn't grab a hold of her but, as soon as I asked for help, it arrived.

It was so unusual for nobody to be around at that time of day, but they didn't appear because I wasn't supposed to go inside my house. I was to go inward and experience the creation of healing.

The connection to breathing has been evident in so many situations in my life. It's the first thing we do when we enter this realm and the last thing we do when we change form. Breathing does change the flow of life force energy entering your body and allows you to create a calmer flow so you can become one and hear the voice of your inner essence.

Thoughts have such power and, just like you can give up with your thoughts, sending vibrations that match that out into the world, you can also send life, vitality and positive energy out too. It's your choice but, whatever one you focus on, it is creating your reality in the physical.

The mother and baby situation was so significant. I believe, as I was holding the bird and allowing the flow of love to surround her, I was also holding a space for my daughter just opposite me in the office; very powerful and humbling.

This experience was created so I could remember the power of my thoughts in any given situation. It's easy to have positive thoughts when everything is going well, but it's being able to consciously align yourself with the flow of the universal energy, no matter what the situation, that is important. Your intentions are crucial, as you are asking for what you want with your intentions. The connection between the injured baby bird and my daughter was clear to me and, in my intentions for the bird I held in my hands to be healed, I wanted the same for my own 'baby bird'. Whilst writing this I was taken back to the first time this happened when my grandson was small. Let's go there now. His name is 'Jermaine'…

Jermaine

After grabbing my tea, I headed into the living room and looked out of the window of the back door. The sun was out, casting its warmth all over the car park. What a beautiful start to the day, I thought. I opened the back door to let in some air and, as I did, a warm breeze flowed through and headed towards the open window opposite, taking with it the old energies accumulated during the night and leaving a fresh new beginning for this fresh new day.

My grandson Jermaine was about a year and a half and had been staying at his Aunty Maxine's house with his Mum. Jermaine had become quite poorly and wasn't himself for a few days. We kept a close eye on him, allowing his body to do what comes naturally, expecting him to get better but, instead, he slowly deteriorated. He was no longer eating or drinking, and his only desire was to sleep, so his Mum called the doctor. The doctor said he'd visit after the surgery closed and diagnosed a type of gastric flu. He was concerned about his lack of fluids and Jermaine's lack of responses and told us that if his condition didn't improve in a few hours, he would have to get him admitted to hospital to be put on a drip and monitored.

We were concerned before but now had been given cause to worry. We tried everything to get him to take fluids, but he refused and just wanted to be left alone to sleep. Jermaine was such a lively boy, full of life and energy. It was sad, seeing him so still and lifeless. I could feel the vibrations of my daughters as they met and entangled with my own, and I had to pull away from the grip of worry to calm myself. Not knowing what to do, I sat down and centred myself in the moment, calming the mind that was drip-feeding me. "Help me, what should I do?" I said.

I looked at this precious little boy and thought how happy he made me, his laugh, his cheeky smile, and the beautiful light that shone out of his eyes, and suddenly felt a strong impulse to just lay him in my arms and love him. I was aware of his Mum sitting opposite as I looked at him, stroking his hair, his face, kissing his forehead and feeling the complete surrender of his little body in my arms. As I focused all my love and attention on him, a cloudy mist began to take over my peripheral vision, until it was eventually blacked out completely by my focus. I was unaware of time or activity but fully focused, praying, wishing, hoping for his recovery. The words of love speaking softly in my head, that 'he is so young and too small to cope, I will take it, transfer it to me', I thought.

I am unsure how long we were in that bubble of love, but I burst back into awareness by movement from his now sweating body. He suddenly sat bolt upright and asked for a 'dwink'. His Mum, who hadn't moved from the chair opposite, jumped up shouting, "He wants a drink!", and, grabbing the beaker from the table, hurriedly gave it to him, just in case he changed his mind. After drinking the beaker-full exceptionally quickly, Jermaine got down from my lap to play with his cars positioned in a line on the coffee table, just as he'd left them. My daughters and I were so relieved, our smiles and vibrations meeting once again, but this time in a dance of relief and delight.

Lydia looked at me and asked, "What did you do?" "I didn't do anything," I replied. "Whatever it was had run its course." But she wasn't convinced and said, "You healed him." I laughed, feeling very uncomfortable with her words, but she insisted and said it again. I told her that was nonsense and to please stop saying that; it was just one of those coincidences and the illness was clearly on its way out when I lay him in my arms.

The doctor was informed and was a bit surprised at the rapid turnaround but did say children are quite resilient. I was shocked and delighted by what happened but wasn't sure what had actually occurred. I definitely wasn't comfortable in taking any credit for it. As I sat there, slowly trying to creep in past the pile of beliefs was a thought that, what if, by some chance, I did manage to heal him? Not a second later the creeping thought was found by the toppling pile of beliefs completely suffocating it with 'who do you think you are?', and I dismissed the possibility that we as humans could be more than we believed we were capable of.

After briefly playing with his cars Jermaine had another drink, something to eat and then slept soundly on the sofa for an hour, before awakening to his bright, vibrant, happy self, as if nothing had happened. The turnaround was amazing.

Once in the sanctuary of my home, I tried to process it. I felt like I wanted to cry, but couldn't, even though the urge was so strong. For a week after the incident, I felt unwell. I couldn't put my finger on it, no symptoms, not ill, just not myself. My family noticed the shine had gone off me and asked me what was wrong, but I couldn't explain it because I didn't know. Lydia said I must have taken on the illness, but my mind quickly dismissed it, laughing at her and asking her not to mention it again, but that creeping thought came back as something in the back of my mind thought it may be a possibility.

When it occurred the second time it could no longer be denied, and I knew it was more than a coincidence. We were at Lisa's wedding reception. Jermaine was still very young, about 3 years old. He had not been himself for a few days, but not unwell. Lydia was in two minds as to whether or not to take him, but knew she could always leave if need be. The music was playing and the atmosphere was lively and the hall was alive with children running around, bits of food and cake being dropped and trodden on as they weaved in and out of the adults on the dance floor.

Jermaine had tried so hard to keep up, caught up in the excitement of it all, his mind active but his body just not responding how he wanted it to, and he soon became too tired and felt unwell. Lydia carried him over to where I was and asked me to do that thing I did last time, heal him. I looked around, hoping nobody close by had heard her words over the sound of the music, as if her words contained a secret that would shock and alienate me from the others.

Life experiences had made me cautious and untrusting, and I'd known from an early age that being different was frowned upon by many and you could get hurt.

I took Jermaine from my daughter, and she followed me out into the hallway. There was a staircase leading to the upper rooms that were not being used, so I sat down on them. Jermaine was wrapped in a woollen cardigan; his forehead was neither hot nor cold and his eyes were shut, but he was not asleep and I could instantly feel the discomfort in his little body. Something inside him had closed down his energy, his cells already on the battlefield, swords at the ready, fighting the organism that invaded him. I think somewhere in the back of my mind a seed had been planted that first time, in Maxine's house, and that seed had grown past the pile of old beliefs that tried to subdue it. It had grown so much that I now knew a positive outcome would occur with Jermaine.

Lydia was hovering around, so I told her to go back to the party, leaving us alone together. I did what I did last time, blocking out everything, the music, the laughter, the people; it was just him and me. I took slow, long breaths in through my nose and out through my mouth. It took me a few moments to adjust and, as I did so, I felt the love start to pour out of my heart area into his. As this love continued to flow there was no separation; we became one. I could feel his cells doubling, tripling by the second and, whatever was causing his discomfort, was being completely taken over by the love pouring into it. I could see the cells dissolving and integrating it and felt the power of the energy as it flowed until, finally, I felt the release and the intense powerful flow beginning to slow down.

Just as that happened, my daughter returned, as if by magic, called by some mysterious force, an impulse inside her letting her know the healing had taken place. At the same time, Jermaine opened his eyes, looked at me, smiled and said, "I want to dance." I thought how funny it was that a Michael Jackson tune had just come on; it was one of Jermaine's favourites. He jumped down from my lap and went running into the hall to find the other kids.

Lydia hugged me with tears running down her face, saying, "You did it again Mum. I knew you could do it." I wanted to cry, to release the feeling inside, but something was blocking it. I wondered if it was it being blocked so I could feel it more intensely before letting it escape, allowing myself a better understanding of what had happened in the process. Or was it the years of being told if I cried I'd be given something to cry for, that was blocking it? Whatever it was, it was something I needed to look into.

Lydia, aware of what happened last time, how I was under the weather for a while, told me I had to find a way to release it, to let it go out into the universe, to be dissolved instead of taking it within. I felt the need to be alone for a while, to process it, so, as they piled into the hall, I sat down on the stairs. I was now sure that I had impacted the wellbeing of my grandson. My love had become more than I ever thought possible. It had the strength and power to heal. We had become one, our energies connecting in a collaboration to dissolve and disintegrate the negative energy that infiltrated his body.

Jermaine was my grandson, and we are connected energetically, the ties of our DNA forever entwined, but if we all come from the same creator, we are all entwined energetically, and then we must all have the power to heal each other. I began to realise that I must consciously open up to allow the love of the creator to flow through me, instead of using my own energy. By focusing on love, not the sentimental anaemic type of love, but the real power of love, the world could be healed.

I wondered what this energy that attacks us is, and can it be prevented? If love can integrate it, is it then a lack of love we feel when we allow it in? Questions, questions, questions. Oh, enough of the questions, I thought… I had not been conscious of the music playing, so consumed in thought, but laughed out loud at the meaningful coincidence and impeccable timing, the words ringing out, sounding so loud and clear as the creator of the world spoke directly to me through Bob, and all I could hear was, "One love, One heart, let's get together and feel alright."

Jermaine reflections

I had been to this place before, where I blanked out the world to be at one with the higher consciousness. I knew this place existed and, in this place, miracles happened, but still I found it hard to believe that I was capable of such a wonderful thing as healing another being; but it was not me personally, it was the energy of love that I had inside me, that we all have inside us. It's our essence, our natural frequency. It was nothing new or, in fact, anything special. It has just been forgotten.

My thoughts of transferring it over to me was a compromise and was not necessary, but my beliefs that if he healed, I would take it on, caused it to become a reality.

I didn't want to seem like a freak, or strange, so I didn't want to entertain the thought of being able to heal. I didn't want to even suggest that I was able to do what the great example Jesus did, but I realised Jesus came to show us we could all do this.

My daughter had been open to the possibility without question, as if she knew we were capable, and she kept on insisting I had a big part in his wellbeing and, as if by magic, she had been summoned to be a witness, once again, to the flow of healing energy.

Was it because Jermaine trusted and loved me that he opened himself up to allow the healing to take place or would it have happened anyway? As we grow, we get bogged down with beliefs that do not serve us but, as a child, we are open and expectant of good things.

Throughout my life I have been given signs and messages from different sources, nature, birds, people, music, and I am always delighted in the way they come to me. We are all given messages but are sometimes distracted by life; they pass us by without noticing. We have to have our eye open to receive them, otherwise we will miss the magic and wonder that is happening around and through us all the time.

This was my first experience with the power of healing, and what a wonderful thing to be able to do. We all have this ability, but run to doctors too quickly to assist in putting more chemicals and toxins into our bodies. I am in no way against medicine, as it plays an important role in our wellbeing, but we must look for more natural ways to administer healing instead. The medicines are designed to take away the issue, and often do, but it also leaves us with other issues to deal with, side effects that are not so beneficial. I remembered a time when I was very young, when I met a boy who changed how I saw medicine, and one who also broke my heart for a while. I would like to take you to my next adventure called 'Kid'…

Kid

I remember the first time I saw Kid. I was about 6 years' old, and I was on my way to the shops with Mum. The sun was out but, as it was still early morning, there was a slight chill to the air, so I had my jacket on and was glad I did. I was holding Mum's hand, skipping along, when a lady came struggling out from a door by the side of the shop. The lady kicked the door open and positioned herself so one of her legs held the door ajar whilst attempting to push the pram out of the door, banging the sides against the door frame. Mum instantly let go of my hand to offer her help, but the lady, although flustered said, "Thank you, I can manage." Mum smiled at her as she looked up from the pram. She fumbled with the keys in her hand and attempted to lock the door with one hand whilst holding onto the pram. The keys fell, hitting the ground, and the lady sighed heavily and thanked her as Mum bent down to pick them up.

Mum made herself known, as she always did. She knew everyone and it was always such a long journey going to and from the shop, as she would stop to chat with everyone she knew. The lady had just moved in above the corner shop and didn't know anyone around the area, so Mum, being Mum, told her where she lived and said to pop in when she wanted to. The pram that had been facing away from us, all of a sudden started to rock and, what I thought was a baby, began to scream in anger about wanting to get out. The lady turned the pram around and there he was, a little boy about my age. He was very angry about being in the pram and kept saying, "I'm not a baby, I want to get out." He had short blond hair and a beautiful face, and eyes that were bright and alive. He stopped shouting as we looked at each other. At that moment a blast of cold air whipped my hair into my face, completely obstructing my view. I grabbed my hair, tucking it behind my ears, and the wind blew it back into my face again, amusing us both, and we both giggled. Still looking at me, the boy threw the blanket that was wrapped around his lower half out of the pram and onto the floor. Then I noticed his legs, he didn't have any, just two stumps where his legs should have been. I should have looked away, but I couldn't stop staring; I'd never seen this before.

After a chat the lady and Mum said goodbye and we proceeded to the shop. I was eager to ask Mum questions and Mum knew they were coming. "Where were his legs?" I asked. "It happens sometimes love," Mum replied. I wanted to know more and asked her, "How does it happen?" Mum explained that Kid's Mum had taken something from the doctor when she was pregnant to stop her being sick and this caused his condition. How can medicine make someone have no legs, I thought, and my questions continued all the way home. Throughout my day, no matter how interested I was in what I was doing or what I was playing with, I couldn't seem to get the image of this boy out of my mind.

We would occasionally see his Mum struggling with him. He was always screaming to get out and his Mum was always telling him why he couldn't. I listened to my Mum talking to Dad about it. She wished she could help in some way but the lady just wouldn't accept any help. One day I was with Mum when a neighbour came along and started talking about him. "It's such a shame, such a handsome looking boy. He would have been a real heartbreaker if he was normal," she said, as if being a heartbreaker was normal and something to be proud of. Mum didn't comment and just made an excuse to leave. Looking back, I can never recall a time where she participated in gossip and I really loved her for that.

I remember, one day, we were outside the balcony where we lived; Mum was sitting on a blanket with my baby sister whilst I ran around on the grass nearby, when his Mum and Kid turned up. Mum welcomed her, telling her to sit down for a while. Kid was screaming to get out, so she picked him up and sat him down on the blanket, telling him to stay there. The next minute he got up on his hands and started running around on his knuckles. I was fascinated and amazed. He looked incredible, and I wanted to do it too. I tried to copy him, but couldn't, as my legs got in the way. Kid's Mum told him to come and sit down, but there was no way. He was in his element, laughing and running around with me. Kid's Mum looked away, feeling a bit embarrassed, until Mum commented on how well he used his arms and how amazing it was to see how fast he was able to run. A slight smile threatened to open up on her face until her mind received the threat and she held it back, just in case.

We were only there a short while before lots of kids started to turn up; they seemed to come from everywhere. A few of them voiced what they saw with no hesitation, whilst some just laughed, pointed and whispered. Kid was aware of them but seemed to take no notice; he appeared far too busy running around to care. Mum asked them nicely to go away and play, but they didn't go very far. After a while Kid began to tire of them and ran at them, shouting. They ran off, screaming in terror. Kid looked round at me, smiling; he had just found a strength he didn't know he had. He enjoyed the power he had in making them run away, only stopping when they thought it was safe enough and would continue watching him from a distance. His Mum tried to stop him but he wasn't listening, so she stood up to leave, but Kid wasn't leaving; he was having far too much fun. He let her get close enough to almost catch him and then would dodge past her. He was so fast and agile and the way he had learnt to swing his lower body was really something to behold. His Mum had such a struggle trying to catch him, much to the amusement of the crowd of kids that were watching from a safe distance.

I didn't see Kid again for years after that. He wasn't allowed to go to the local schools and had to go to a special school. The next time I saw him I was about 12 years old. I was skating by the pub on the corner just outside my flats. I loved skating there as the paving was level and smooth and I could practise my turns really well. I was waiting for my friend to arrive; she had agreed to meet me there after she finished her dinner. I had just finished a turn when I heard a loud thud land on the car bonnet nearest to me. When I looked up, there was Kid. He really was a beautiful sight. His face was as handsome as ever and his arms and shoulders looked strong. With a confident tone he said, "I remember you," and I smiled as I told him, "I remember you too." He said, "I can't remember your name, though." "It's Frances, but my friends call me Frankie," I replied, "what's yours?" He chuckled as he replied, "'Thlid Kid', even my friends call me 'Thlid Kid'." I didn't understand and asked him why? He explained that while his Mum was pregnant with him, she had taken a drug called Thalidomide for morning sickness and it had caused his deformity, and that's why he was nicknamed 'Thlid Kid'. A feeling crept into my stomach, squeezing it tightly, and I said, "I don't like that name, so I will just call you Kid." He shook his head, "I don't care, it don't matter to me." While I skated around near him he told me that the doctor said he wouldn't live to be 19. I was very surprised and shocked and asked him, "How does the doctor know?" He replied, "We don't last long; most of us die at birth, so I suppose I am the lucky one."

Kid had tied thick bits of cloth around his hands to protect them from the gravel and stones on the ground. He said his hands were bleeding really badly 'til he came up with the idea of covering them. He had been given a wheelchair to get around but refused to get in it. He was always getting into trouble at school as they insisted he use it, but he refused. He enjoyed the freedom of movement and loved being able to jump the way he could. He listened intently as I told him how incredible I thought it was, the way he could jump up on the car the way he did, and how I didn't know anyone else that could do it. He said his Mum tried to keep him in for his safety and kept the door locked, but he was really good at escaping and got out all the time. Kid asked me what it was like to skate, and I told him it felt like I was flowing and floating on air when the ground was smooth. It felt like freedom and we both resonated with that feeling and smiled at each other, fully enjoying the moment. I received a great idea. "Why don't you put my skates on," I said. He liked that idea, so I quickly sat down to take my skates off for him to try. Eager to try them, Kid jumped down from the car bonnet and was now sitting with me on the ground. I had just taken my skates off when my friend turned the corner. As fast as a blink of my eye Kid jumped back on the car bonnet with a heavy thud, shouting, "See ya," and was gone in a flash, lost amongst the cars parked by the side of the road.

I saw him rarely after that, but heard he was getting into a lot of trouble around the area. He was over-confident now and feeling his power and loved the attention he was getting from the other boys. I knew Kid wasn't bad, he just wanted to fit in, to belong and be accepted. I would listen as the boys would talk amongst themselves about getting him to scare people, and even hit them on occasions. Kid had extremely strong arms, being both his arms and legs, and he could appear out of nowhere. He could jump up on a car roof and punch someone very easily and get away, he learnt to use everything around him to his advantage and was so fast, they were unable to catch him. I could see the boys were using him; they were not real friends and told them so, but they didn't listen and would taunt me about loving a monkey boy.

On this one occasion I saw one of the boys talking to him and could tell he was up to no good. I approached them and, speaking to Kid, told him not to listen to him and not to be used. I told Kid the boy was not his friend, as a friend wouldn't call him by that name. The boy turned around in anger, gave me a quick sidewards glance, then said to Kid, "Don't listen to her, she calls you 'Thlid Kid' behind your back…" My heart fell into my stomach with a thud, as I looked around at the boy in disbelief, and then straight into Kid's eyes, denying every last letter that made up that horrible word. But the look on his face, and the fog that blocked out the light in his eyes, said that the snake had bitten and the poisonous lie was seeping into his bloodstream at a rapid rate. I tried to stop it. "Take that back, you liar!" I said to the boy, every part of me wanting to kick the crap out of him. The boy suddenly had a change of heart. "She didn't say it," he said, but the change of heart came too late, as the lie flowing through Kid's body had already reached its destination. Kid didn't know what to believe, so he believed the worst. He didn't know what a real friend was. All his life, experiences had shown him a world that didn't respond well to him. Why should I be any different? Kid turned to disappear again and, as he ran off across the cars, he left a trail of broken letters that made up the words, "I don't care anyway." All I could do was watch him go. I turned to speak to the boy, but he was disappearing, just like Kid. I turned back in Kid's direction, suddenly feeling so incredibly alone and watched him getting smaller. I looked away, briefly blinking fast to stop the tears and, as I looked in Kid's direction again, I observed that brief moment in time where he thought it was safe to put his hand to his face to wipe away his tears, and my heart was truly broken.

I didn't see him again for a few years after that. He and his Mum had moved away suddenly and nobody knew where they had gone, but his reputation for bad behaviour travelled far and I was always hearing things about him. I suppose it was easy for him to claim that title as he was very unique; he stood out from the crowd and was easily recognisable. One day I was with a friend in Camden, visiting her aunt. We had taken a short cut through a side road to the shop, when I saw him. My heart started beating rapidly and I said out loud, "I know him," as I quickly walked toward him. Kid was sitting by the side of the road, drinking a can of beer. As I approached, I noticed the cloths on his hands were worn out, ripped and ragged from the years of constant pounding of his hands as they hit the ground. His hair was messy and wild and, as I approached, he looked up and our eyes met. I know for sure, for that one pure, divine moment, both our souls danced in joy and recognition of each other. "Hi Kid, do you remember me?" I said, but instead of a smile he turned away from me, and I noticed the once handsome face was now contorted and lined and wondered how that could be, as he was still so young. I tried to get him to acknowledge my presence, but I couldn't get close. It was as though he put an invisible force field around himself, a bubble to keep himself safe, but it didn't keep him safe, it just kept people away.

I asked him again if he remembered me and, without even giving me a second look, replied, "NO," as he squeezed the half-drunk can of beer in half, forcefully pushing the liquid out of the opening and throwing it angrily to the ground. There was a couple on the other side of the road, looking over and, as his eyes caught sight of them, he sneered and said, "Watch this," as he ran towards them, shouting and screaming. They both looked terrified and started running up the road, as Kid jumped up onto a car and continued to go from car to car, screaming and chasing them. I waited for him to come back but he never did and, as I stood there, I realised he was gone again and my heart felt like the half-drunk beer can, crushed in the gutter with the left-over liquid seeping out.

I had wrestled with my emotions over and over that day, and the lie, and had tried to make it right, but there was nothing I could do. I realised he had made a choice to believe the lie. I hadn't hurt him, his own mind did that. I couldn't begin to understand the difficulties he faced day in and day out, the looks, the sniggers, the names, living in a world that laughed and taunted instead of embracing uniqueness. I was able to keep quiet if I didn't want to share my differences, but Kid's were on show for everyone to see.

I believe there were many others that met Kid along his journey that felt the same way as I did, people that saw his love for life, admiring the way he adapted to his condition, not just making the best of it, but learning to create a new way of being out of it. I wondered if Kid had known, at that time, the love and admiration I had for him, would he have felt so alone? If only Kid could see what I saw when I looked at him. We only had fleeting moments together, but those moments held a lifetime of feeling inside them. I realised it's not how long you are with someone, or the length of time you've known them. It's the deepness and connection of a moment together that creates and keeps a bond. When I look back, I believe Kid was my first love and he may not have been classed as normal in the eyes of others, but he certainly was my heartbreaker.

A few months later I heard Kid passed away. I knew as soon as he left his body the truth was revealed, and he knew for sure how I felt about him. He knew the moment I saw him running on the grass that I felt pure love. The feeling I had for him was never pity, just pure admiration for his love of freedom, his longing to explore and his willingness to get out into the world and live it on his terms, be it right or wrong in the eyes of others.

Although I felt great sadness at first, the day I heard the news, it was quickly replaced by a feeling of immense happiness, as a strong breeze loosened some of my tied-back hair blowing it into my face, obstructing my view. I tucked it behind my ears and the wind blew it out again. I giggled out loud and felt a warmth rise up in my stomach, as I knew for sure his energy hadn't died, it had just changed form, and Kid was letting me know he was floating, flowing and feeling true freedom again.

Kid Reflections

From an early age, Kid learnt to look for a reaction from people when seeing his legs. As he threw the blanket off, he observed my reaction, taking in the shock I felt. He was looking at my reaction from his own eyes, making his own conclusions from his prior experiences, but, for me it was only shock, nothing more, and once over the initial shock, I could see him in his true light.

Kid's Mum must have been through a lot of negative experiences and clearly felt very protective of him. She found it hard to accept any help, but there were good people that could have helped and supported her, had she just opened up and learnt to trust a little. I believe she must have asked for help in her mind, so many times, and then Mum came along. Mum would have been a good friend to her, but her life experiences and her thoughts prevented her from accepting the very thing she was clearly asking for. We sometimes keep out the very thing we really want because of our thoughts and beliefs about it.

On that first meeting with Kid, it was the simple act of the wind blowing my hair in my face and us giggling together that made the connection and the sharing of a moment that lasted a lifetime.

We trust that the man-made chemicals we put in our bodies as medicine are good for us, and I am not in any way against medicine, but the side effects of some of these toxins have to be recognised. We have to consider the long-term effects of everything we put into our bodies, as cancer is on the increase, despite advancements in medicines.

When my younger sister Dee was very little she suffered with pneumonia. She was so ill, she had to go into hospital. I had seen how the medicines they gave her saved her life, and was thankful that they had. I also witnessed how Dee could turn from a calm, loving child, to one we didn't recognise. When given penicillin, she became aggressive and angry very quickly, which was so out of character.

Kid didn't want to be confined to a pram, a wheelchair or metal legs, he wanted to run around. Kid wanted the freedom to express himself and move himself around in the best way he could. His environment, his Mum, the teachers, the doctors with the best intentions in the world, all kept telling him he was disabled and insisted he lived his life confined to a wheelchair, despite him being able get around easier on his hands. It just wasn't the 'done' thing to be or look different.

I believe, if he had confined himself to a wheelchair, both adults and children would have reacted differently to him. They could have felt sorry for him or even pity, but Kid didn't want those feelings from anyone. He wanted the same thing we all want, freedom to be and accepted just as we are.

The statement that Kid would have been a heartbreaker if he was normal, was untrue. There are many ways to break someone's heart and there are no 'normal' people, we are all different.

The boy that told the lie to Kid did so much damage with that lie, but I suppose, if I look at it another way, how was I to know whether that boy was a friend to Kid or not? I was judging him the same as the others, but I didn't know what they were talking about and I only had my perspective to go on. Maybe the boy was upset with me for saying he was using Kid and he reacted without thinking properly.

It was up to Kid as to what he did with the lie and Kid only had his young experiences to go by.

Kid learnt to say he didn't care as a defence. He'd said them so often, the words just slipped off his tongue with ease, without real thought as to whether they had any truth behind them.

Was the doctor right in telling Kid he would die before he was 19? Was this helpful or not? We all know we will die at some point, and none of us know when that point will come. Did this give Kid the determination he had to live life any way he wanted, as he saw no real future past this age, or was it a death sentence that prevented him from creating the future he wanted?

All Kid really wanted was to be loved and accepted, but his experiences of the unaccepting nature of people around him made him adapt himself to his environment and found power in becoming something to be scared of, instead. Many people have found this same power as they journey through life.

My friend would have been just as welcoming to Kid as I was, but he had already decided that she wasn't going to be receptive to him so he didn't give her a chance to prove him wrong. Kid didn't know he could have had two good friends.

Kid used his new-found power to impress his so-called friends, but ended up just being used. Moving further and further away from what he really wanted, until the gap was so wide, he felt it couldn't be filled again, finding some form of comfort in drinking to escape, as many people do.

From as far back as I can remember, I have had a deep knowing there was far more going on than what I could see, hear, smell, taste or touch, and had always wondered where people go when they die. I was told they went to a place called 'heaven' and imagined heaven to be somewhere in the sky. But I know we are all energy, everything is energy and, once the essence of your energy leaves the physical body, it merges with all that is and flows freely in its entirety, uniting with the energy that creates worlds. The day I found out Kid had passed away, Kid was ready to let me know he was home. Playing with my hair to remind me of a time we shared where two children met, creating a connection that lasted way beyond the physical realms.

Knowing Kid changed me in a big way; I not only observed others and their reactions to him but was also so thankful for the upbringing my parents gave me. I didn't see him in the same way. He fascinated me the way he went against the norm and was so determined to be himself. Kid would not live confined to a wheelchair just so people could accept him; he stood in his truth, despite it hurting him. This takes me back to a defining time in my life. Come with me to a story called 'Father Christmas…'

Father Christmas

My life up until school was magical. It was one big adventure and my imagination ran wild. Mum and Dad would always try to accommodate me with any props such as blankets, sheets, bits of wood and materials. My home life was full of fun and laughter and I had complete freedom to express myself in any way I wanted. I'd wear Mum's ribbons she used for dressmaking around my forehead like a native American Indian and would tie her scarves around my wrists so they hung down, exaggerating my arm movements, I liked their flow as I danced around the room.

I was looking forward to school; I was confident and made friends easily. I had grown up around lots of children as my Mum and Dad both worked when I was young so, from an early age, I was looked after by a lady called Nanny Crane, (a great name for a nanny). The nursery rhyme, the lady that lived in the shoe, always reminded me of her as her house was always full of children. Nanny Crane lived just across the road from us in a two-storey terraced house. She had a round face with pink cheeks, she was plump and cuddly and was always wiping her hands on her apron. Nanny Crane was kind but firm and never smacked anyone, although she did threaten to on rare occasions. She had learnt that by using the tone of her voice and matching it up with the fear of an imagined consequence she could manage to keep us all in order, letting us know when we had gone too far and needed to stop.

Mum had returned to work when I was about a year and a half. My sister Caz was five years older than me and went to Nanny Crane's for a while with me before starting school. Caz would never let anything happen to me; she absolutely adored me. I started school in the September, an eager, excited child, full of life and confidence. As we walked up to the school gates, I wondered why it had such a high fence around it. It's funny how I'd never really noticed it before and, for a few moments, I felt a confined feeling well up in me, but relaxed again when Mum explained it was only there to keep us all safe.

Once inside the school gates I felt a bit anxious and overwhelmed at the number of children, noise and the newness of my surroundings, but the reassuring clasp of Mum's hand in mine helped me to centre myself and feel safe again. I had so wanted to wear my scarves around my wrists this morning but Mum said I wasn't allowed to in school; it was the first time she had refused me. The first few months at school were a breeze. I settled in well and became popular very quickly. I had my own mind and made playtime fun, always making up new games that everyone seemed to want to play. I really enjoyed learning and I liked my teachers, but I didn't like being made to hold hands and to line up.

It's funny how quickly things can change, how one incident can so completely alter your life. That morning I had been skipping along, holding my Mum's hand on the way to school. It was a cold, fresh morning, snow was due anytime now, and it was nearly Christmas. The school halls and classrooms were being decorated with paper streamers and lights, and a big Christmas tree sat in the main assembly hall. As the bell was rung for playtime, we all streamed out of the building into the playground and I saw my sister Caz as the adjoining door to the junior playground was opened for the teacher to go through, and I called her. She came over and gave me a quick hug before the teacher closed the door, separating us again. My group of friends and I headed underneath the shed, and one of the girls told us excitedly what Father Christmas was bringing her. She had been good for weeks now and even wrote him a letter, along with a list, and my friends all discussed leaving oranges, biscuits and little treats for him. Then the other kids started pitching in with what they were getting as I watched and listened.

We hadn't been raised to believe in Father Christmas. We were told there was no Father Christmas and any presents you received were from your Mum and Dad, family and friends, and Christmas was a time to remember to be kind and generous to each other. The gifts received depended only on what could be afforded at the time and had nothing to do with deserving them. We were happy with this knowledge and, even at an early age, understood the value of the truth. I felt happy to share the truth with my friends and spoke up confidently, giving them details of who really supplied their presents, but their reaction startled me. They all insisted I was wrong; their belief in Father Christmas was so strong. It shocked me how upset they seemed to be, their need to believe he was real was so apparent, but I was adamant that they should know the truth and told them that they would only get presents if their parents could afford it, even if they had been good. One of the girls started crying, the others cuddling her. They led her to the teacher watching over us in the playground and, as I stood under the shed alone, I could see them pointing at me.

The teacher came over to me with the others in tow and asked me to stop telling them about Santa, but I told her it was the truth. By this time a few other children had joined the crying girl in her misery, and it seemed as if every child in the playground had come to see what was happening and they all appeared to be unhappy with me. This was a new feeling for me and one I didn't enjoy. A kid shouted, "Take it back and stop lying!" but I said, "No" and, with that, the teacher marched me inside the building. After a brief conversation I was handed over to another teacher. She sat me down and told me I mustn't go around saying things like that because the other children believe in Father Christmas, and I am upsetting them. I was told I could go back outside to play but I must not talk about Santa Claus not being real. I didn't understand this; I was only telling the truth.

So, I sat outside the Head Master's office. It's funny how some details are fuzzy when you look back, while others are really clear and appear to have little relevance to the experience. I recall sitting there, waiting for him to appear, looking down at the parquet flooring. The wood was extra shiny and I noticed how the pieces locked together in a wood-like jigsaw puzzle, but made no picture. Then I started picking at the little blue flowers with tiny dots in the middle on my dress and noticed how, as they reached the hemline, some got cut in half. I was extremely anxious waiting for the Head's arrival. Only bad children go to see the Head Master, and with my imagination working overtime, he soon became a monster in my mind. When he arrived, he was surprisingly nice and explained very clearly to me about how the other children felt about Father Christmas. The Head Master told me I was right, it's not true, but the other children don't know that and believe in him, and it's not for me to tell them the truth, it's for their parents to do that, so he asked me not to mention it again. I didn't understand, but was so overwhelmed by it all, I agreed and was taken back to my class.

As I entered the class I could feel the coldness of the others. They were still upset with me and I saw the cold looks directed at me as I sat down. I felt condemned, an outcast, for the first time in my life. We were still very young so, when the bell went at the end of the day, the teacher would stand at the class doorway, ready to hand you back when your Mum or Dad arrived. My Dad was one of the first to arrive. At that time, he was working as a long-distance lorry driver and was home until his next haul. I ran, sinking my whole body into his legs, and he picked me up. I was so happy to see him and pushed my face into his neck and was quickly comforted by the smell of tobacco and tea. As we headed into the playground, he asked me about my day, and I told him it was a bad one. As I explained, he asked questions and stopped walking towards the gate. I could hear the tone in his voice change, it became lower and more primal, and the feel of his words and the energy seeping out of him began to frighten me.

Heading back into the building, he marched straight up to my teacher, who was talking to one of the mothers, and demanded an explanation as one of the other teachers hurried off to get the Head. The hallway was alive with parents collecting their kids as the teacher tried to explain to my Dad, who was at this point becoming more and more irate by what he heard. The Head arrived and suggested talking in his office but Dad demanded an explanation right where he was, and now. He listened intently whilst the head spoke but was completely dissatisfied with the explanation. Now it was his turn. He was angry at how they had handled and managed the incident. He said it wasn't right that just because the majority of children believed in a fairy tale handed down to them by their parents, that this should impact negatively on me, his daughter, who, for telling the truth, had been made to feel like she's done something wrong and, to make matters even worse, was being told to hide the truth so others could feel better in their lie, and all this from people that are supposed to be teaching the children.

He agreed that children should be allowed to use their imagination and to dream but said it should come from their own imagination and not something handed down by their parents only to be exposed later on in life as a lie. He asked how you'd expect your children to believe you when you tell them lies. He asked what value there was in telling a child that, if they are good, Santa will bring them the present they want. What about people that just can't afford to give their children the presents they deserve? How does that affect a child, thinking they are not good enough because some fictional character didn't bring them what they wanted, even if they have been good? He said God only knows why you tell them a strange man climbs down your chimney to leave presents for them. What about God? Will they still have faith in an unseen power once they realise you've lied to them for years about the mythical Father Xmas? He said, "Why don't you encourage truth, generosity and love, not just at Christmas, but every day?" My Dad told his truth with passion and conviction and the Head really didn't know what to say in response, but muttered and stumbled, going over old ground, but not making any real headway as the sea of faces stood around, listening. As we walked out of the school's main building, hand in hand, he looked down at me, winked and, giving my hand a squeeze, said, "I think we told them what's what," and I smiled back at him.

I felt comforted and safe, hearing it all once again as it was relayed to Mum. My Dad was very opinionated and had his own set of rules that he lived by, and this incident would play over and over in his head for days, even weeks, until he had processed, dissected and dissolved every last bit, until finally spitting out the last remaining pips… those pips, landing firmly in my mind, would begin to develop with me as I grew. My life at school changed completely from that day. Children can be so cruel, but it's mostly learnt behaviour. They are always listening, even when they seem engrossed in their toys, they are picking up the frequencies, the energy around them from their environments. I had fallen out of favour with both children and teachers. My Dad had embarrassed them to the point of no return, and their egos were bruised. I felt their coldness, I felt their disconnection and, in my loneliness, my vibration lowered and I attracted more of the same in the form of bullying and I became the butt of jokes, jibes and pokes. I told the teacher, who dismissed it as playing, but I knew the difference. This hurt and it wasn't fun.

It's funny how our little thoughts and fears take over. I dared not tell my Dad; he would come up and make a scene, making things worse. In any case, he was away a lot, driving the lorries. If I told Mum, she would tell Dad, so I kept it to myself, hoping it would go away, but it never did. I became a nightmare for Mum, who had two other children to look after as well at the time. Sunday nights I would start feeling sick, wanting to stay home where I was safe, loved and free.

The school had started to lock the gates as too many times I had left the school to go home, crossing a busy road on the way. Mum had a meeting with the head to discuss options as it was becoming a real safety issue. Mum would hand me over to the teacher and, as soon as she was preoccupied, I'd seize the opportunity, slipping out and heading home.

One morning my Mum had forgotten to give the teacher my dinner money, realising when she was half-way down the road. She came back into the classroom to see the boy sitting next to me with his hand gripping my hair, trying to hit my head against the wall. She shouted at the boy to stop and told the teacher off. For a few days the bullying stopped, only to increase a few days later, so I resigned myself to the fact that nobody could help me. I retracted inwards, trying to make myself as small and less noticeable as possible, but the bullying got worse.

Confusion set in. Why had this happened? Why had the children, my friends and the teachers behaved like this? Why did they shut their eyes to the truth and hate me for revealing it? I felt a lump in my throat. How was I going to be 'me' if I couldn't tell my truth? Yes, when I rode my bike, it was a horse, and yes, when I wore beads around my forehead I was an Indian princess, but that was for the moment, I knew I could be anything I wanted and often was, but I also knew when it was time to be me. This was different and I didn't understand it.

I became disinterested in learning, school already teaching me a valuable lesson and I no longer believed in its structure and what it stood for. I adapted by splitting my energy. At school I was quiet, I would sit myself as close to a window as possible and spend as much time as I could looking out at the sky, watching the birds and daydreaming. I had learnt that they didn't want or appreciate the truth, so, I observed. As soon as I was out of the gates and heading home, I was lively, happy and confident… I expressed.

One morning, just after Mum handed me over, the gates had been locked and I slipped out of class. The teacher no longer ran after me. She knew I couldn't get out and would end up coming back, and the amount of noise I made was not worth restraining me. I ran to the fence, running my hands along the metal as if I was trying to find a hole big enough to crawl through, and came to the gate. the gate, that had once made me feel safe, had now become my prison and the staff and inmates were not friendly. I could feel freedom through the diamond-shaped holes in the metal cage that trapped me and, as I pushed my fingers through the metal, I gripped it like a claw and found some leverage, instinctively my little feet found the diamonds beneath me, and I used both to push myself upwards. As I continued upwards, I realised I was climbing to freedom and a feeling of excitement rose up in me and I laughed as I continued to rise, slowly reaching the top. I didn't know how to get over. I put one leg over, straddling the top, but fear erupted in me, taking over my joy. It was so far down, and I was wobbling. I was stuck between two worlds, so I stopped, doing nothing. I looked at the school building, the classrooms with their lights on, and then turned my head and looked down the road. I could see my Mum, something inside me kicked in and I found my grip with my foot on the other side, the descent becoming easier as my joy returned, and I flowed effortlessly to the bottom. I ran a little to catch up with Mum, staying far enough away from her not to notice me and walked behind her all the way home.

As my Mum went through the process of opening the front door, stepping in, turning round to close the door behind her, there I stood looking at her with a smile on my face. Even though Mum took me back I somehow felt alright. Everyone was shocked and horrified and meetings were arranged. My Dad was home for the meeting and when the Head told me how dangerous it was for me to climb the fence, I looked at my Dad and, although his face was still, his eyes were smiling and I knew even though I could have hurt myself badly, it was still an accomplishment.

That day they realised the extent of my unhappiness and things were put in place. I didn't climb the fence again; I didn't need to. the cage couldn't hold me and was no longer a threat, but I remained quiet. I now felt different from the others, like I didn't belong, but I had a new-found strength and an inner knowing that, if life at school became unbearable, I had everything I needed inside me, ready and waiting to lift me up. The diamonds would assist me as I rose to the top. The wobble would make me focus and all I had to do was choose which way to go.

Father Xmas reflections

This experience, at such a young impressionable age, really set the stage for how I learned at school. Even at that young age I knew, in my heart, that my Dad was right. It doesn't matter how innocent the story about Father Christmas may be, I still believe a child should still know it is a made-up story and your loved ones buy your presents.

You don't have to use force to correct a child. When you learn how to use the tone, pitch and frequencies of your voice, you can make them feel the urgency of what you are saying. I can remember knowing how much I could push a boundary by the response I was getting energetically. Did you know when your parents or caregiver were serious about what they were saying, or whether there was a little more leeway before it got serious?

I was enjoying school and being with the other children up until the incident. School puts you in a box that you have to fit into, otherwise you are seen as a nuisance. Instead of embracing differences, you are alienated. How lovely to go to a school where they embrace your uniqueness, your natural talents and gifts and learn how to become better teachers by learning from your pupils. We are forever growing and learning, and there was a massive learning curve for everyone in that incident, if you have the eyes to see.

We have to be conscious of how we are raising our children wanting our children to be truthful, but then showing them how to lie. We are the examples, the elders, the parents, family, teachers and friends.

Telling the truth, but being condemned for it, impacted me negatively and gave me the wrong impression of school and all it stood for. At the time it was painful, but now I know it was an evolving experience. After all, in not fitting you have no option but to stand out.

Children don't always confide in their parents about bullying for this exact reason. They only have to receive a negative response once from an action and they will make the association, preferring to suffer in silence, hoping it goes away or gets better.

Once I realised the fence couldn't keep me in, I had an inner comfort, a knowing I could climb it and go home. In my pursuit for freedom,

I received the help I needed to get everyone on track again, but, by this time, I had come to my conclusions and was no longer interested in school, the children or in learning what they were trying to teach me.

The first lie is to tell them a man called Father Christmas comes down your chimney, and all the rest of the things they are led to believe, and they believe you. When do you tell them you've been lying to them all these years? When they are old enough to know the truth? If they can't trust us on things like this, we shouldn't wonder why they can't trust us on more important things.

If I hadn't known the truth I would have been left wondering and confused as to why that mean boy that pulled and taunted me in class, received a new bike for Christmas, despite not being good.

How does a little child feel when Santa doesn't bring them the presents they asked for, despite being good? Is this story only for the wealthy?

The spirit of Christmas should be about giving, caring, sharing and loving each other, and this is something we should practice all year. I like the giving and receiving of presents at Christmas and the food, etc, but I feel it's time for a different story….

We all have our own opinions on what God is; we have different names and ways of looking at who and what God represents. Writing this, I am taken back to an experience I had whilst trying to figure out what my thoughts were and, in my searching, what I did find was the feeling, the frequency of it. Let's go visit 'God's House'…

God's House

We were not a religious family. We were raised believing in a higher power, a guiding force, which was much more powerful than we could ever imagine. I suppose, if asked, my Dad would have said he was Christian, but he never attended church and didn't agree with all their principles and ways. He read the Bible, taking from it what he saw in it, in his own way and with his own perspective. I would have called my Dad a spiritual man who followed no one, much preferring to tread his own path, be it right or wrong in the eyes of others. Dad was in tune with his own inner guidance and made decisions based on how he felt, rather than what he thought about something. I was never encouraged or discouraged to follow any religious ways and was left to find my own way to what we called 'God'.

One day I was in my friend's house watching a film and there was a part that was filmed in a church. There were people clapping, laughing and dancing in the aisles and, watching them, I got goose bumps all over my body and, as their soulful voices rang out, I felt completely overwhelmed and emotional as the vibrations rippled out and touched me, uplifting my soul in a way I'd never felt before. I thought that if people felt like this about God, I wanted in. I wanted to go to church and experience coming together with others in this way. When I reached home Mum and Dad were in the living room, and I asked them if I could go to church. They said, "Of course you can," but asked where I got the idea from, as it seemed so out of the blue. I didn't explain myself properly and just said I wanted to try it. I suppose if I had explained what I'd seen on TV, they could have advised me, but I think they would have let me experience it for myself anyway, allowing my experience to shape my own perception.

I was still very young, so it was arranged that I'd go with a family friend who took their kids to church every Sunday, and they were more than happy to take me. Their children attended Sunday school in the morning before services, so I was to go along too. At Sunday school I settled down in my seat and glanced at my black patent shiny shoes and white knee-length socks. I smiled as I looked at the lovely little dress Mum had made; it had a hair band to match. I had wanted to look especially nice; after all, I was visiting God today. We were given a picture of Jesus in his manger to colour in and the teacher told us all about his birth and his death. I was horrified at the brutality of those that caused it, but I was also curious as to what Jesus was doing in the in-between bit, between his birth and death. I asked the teacher and was told he was a carpenter, he made furniture. "Yes, but what else? What about before that?" I asked, "did he go anywhere? Who were his friends? What did he play with?" The teacher dismissed my questions as unimportant, so they remained unanswered and travelled around in my mind. I wondered; did he make camps? Did he rescue birds? And was his bike a horse?

I was excited as I entered the church doors. I breathed in deeply, taking in the atmosphere, filling myself up with it. Looking around in wonder, it was beautiful. I noticed how the light shone through the image of Jesus in the stained-glass window and looked around at the other windows for the image of God. It felt special being in the house where God lives but wondered where he was. We were all seated when the vicar came in. I looked at him lovingly, seeing him as one of God's best friends. He looked directly at me and I smiled, but he didn't smile back. Perhaps he didn't see me, I thought. As he spoke, the warmth, the passion and the love I expected were replaced by judgment and a tone of voice with no depth. It felt as though the vicar was recalling something he'd read but not really understood, and the love, well, I didn't feel any. I felt no connection to the horror of this wrath that he said God had for me. The vicar seemed to go on forever, and it didn't take long before I started to get restless and shifty, moving about and openly yawning. We were seated at the front, and he must have sensed what I was feeling as he kept looking at me. 'Ah, now he sees me!'

'Bring on the dancing and singing and let God appear', I thought, 'I can't wait to get to the good part', but it never came. When we stood up for hymns it was lifeless, it lacked feeling, passion, and it was soulless, just words from a book that seemed to mean nothing and lacked any energy. I knew deep in my stomach that this stiff, starchy, judgemental kind of feeling was not the God I'd come to know and love. I didn't really know or understand what God was, but I had felt it… I knew it was a light feeling, a feeling of flow. It was vibrancy, uplifting, happiness, Joy and Love…Yes, it was Love.

At that time, I didn't realise that God was everywhere and in everything, God was in all things, in the leaf of a tree, in the mountains and streams, in a baby's cry and in the smile on a face. I didn't need to look for God, I had God inside me. I could see, touch and connect with the energy in the stillness of my mind. I had access to the flow, the light, the energy that is always flowing to me, as it is to all of us. This is what Jesus, and many others, came to teach us. They opened themselves up fully to receive the flow, allowing the energy to flow through them. They were great examples of conscious connection to the one and only source of all creation.

I had come to church to find God and to sing and dance in appreciation of this powerful energy force, but in that search, on that day, I came to the conclusion that the vicar had forgotten to tell him we were coming as he wasn't at home and was out having fun somewhere else.

God's House reflections

I loved the way my Mum and Dad allowed me the freedom to find my own way to God. Giving me the foundation, the energy, the life force as a seed for me to develop and grow in my own personal way.

Watching the movie had given me a feeling that I wanted to explore; I wanted to sing, clap and feel the coming together with others in a high frequency vibration, a dance of love and appreciation for the joy of life, but the reality was very different for me and didn't match my vision and expectation.

The Sunday school teacher had taken my questions as not important, but as a child, all questions are important. I would love to know, even now as an adult, what Jesus did as a child.

It's funny how, despite smiling at the vicar and looking at him lovingly, he appeared not to notice me, but as soon as I started to shift around and yawn in my seat he noticed me, for all the wrong reasons.

Of course, God was with us in the church, because we are all sparks of divine light in bodies and our perceptions of God are different, and we all feel the energy in our own ways. For me, I want to celebrate, dance and sing in appreciation of all the things that I experience as, even in the darkness, the pain and the grief, when you have the eyes to see and the heart to feel, the energy of love is always present.

Even at that young age, God, for me, was a beautiful feeling full of Love. I felt the energy in the wind, the sun, the birds and the trees. The energy of God breathed and lived in fun and happiness and had never appeared to me as a harsh, brutal, conditional feeling. The only time in my life where I thought differently was when I had replaced those loving thoughts that I knew to be truth with ones that were judgmental; cutting myself off from the flow of love that was always unconditionally flowing to me.

I remember the first time I really felt cut off from source as a child. Of course, the unconditional love I'd come to know had not gone anywhere; it was the feelings and thoughts about me that disconnected me. When I remember back to this day, I can see how amazing my parents really were in their teachings, and this is a great example of the many different ways you can teach a child without using force. Let's go to 'My Scream'…

My Scream

I t was the six weeks' holidays at last! I loved it! The freedom I felt from the restrictions of school and all its rules caused my heart to be full of joy, and I lived each day in eager anticipation for the day ahead. I rode the waves of happiness throughout the daylight hours, eagerly excited in every moment and every night I would slowly come down from the high vibration, falling peacefully to sleep. Each new day was the same; it was thirsty work being this happy. As we played and laughed the ice cream man took full advantage of the holidays and the hungry kids that swarmed around his van. It was always the same van with the same tune. We would hear him coming as 'somewhere over the rainbow' vibrated out in the distance, giving us enough time to run inside for our money before he parked up. It was funny how a tune was able to disrupt any game we were playing, with everyone running in different directions, disappearing the moment the tune rang out. I was rarely able to get one. Mum had four children to cater for and just couldn't afford it, but I would always run into the house to ask, just in case. I would watch as my friends' ice-creams melted and dripped down the cone enticingly. How I wished I could taste it.

I understood that we didn't have the money, but it upset me that, whenever I asked, it was always 'No'. At the time, I didn't realise it upset Mum more than it ever did me. Mum had to refuse, not just once, but four times, as we all ran to the house, one by one, but I was too young at the time to grasp or even comprehend. 'Maybe today will be different,' I thought, running into the house to ask. 'Mum's ship may have come in,' but it hadn't and Mum said, "Not today love," and walked off into the living room. I was fed up with not being able to have one; that day I really wanted one. I wanted to taste the cream and feel the sauce on my tongue, catching it just before it dripped down the cone, so I sat on the second step of the stairs right opposite the kitchen with my elbows perched on my knees, my hands under my chin and a frown between my eyes.

As I sat there, hoping that my sad face would suddenly make money appear, I looked at the washed plates drying on the draining board and my eyes caught a glimpse of the shiny edge of Mum's tin that she kept on the top shelf of the cupboard in the kitchen. The tin was used to put change in that she needed to pay the milkman, and I remembered this as I sat there. 'Mum does have money, she's just being mean!', I thought (but Mum didn't have a mean bone in her body). I sat there, trying to justify the thought going round in my head, and the more I thought about it, the more I convinced myself. Double-checking that Mum was still seated in the living room, I proceeded to climb onto the counter to where the tin was. Grabbing a handful of ten penny bits I jumped down and quickly ran out of the house. My heart was pounding but I was excited. I had money for an ice cream. Mum would never know; there were loads of coins in that tin. As I approached the van, I looked around to check that my brother and sisters were not around. They would definitely tell if they saw me. The coast was clear, so I quickly paid for the ice cream, collected my change and ran round to the back of the flats to eat it. At last, we were alone, but the excitement I had felt started to melt away. I looked at the ice cream and a funny, weird feeling rose up in me from my stomach. It was a horrible, tight feeling and suddenly the ice cream lost its appeal. I felt bad for stealing the money, but what could I do? It was too late now and the ice cream was starting to drip, so I proceeded to gobble it up, getting rid of the evidence as fast as I could. It didn't taste how I thought it would. I didn't enjoy it at all, apart from it giving me brain freeze from eating it too fast. I knew it wasn't right, it felt so wrong, and after finishing it I asked God to forgive me.

Later that day, I carefully waited for the right time and carefully put the change back in the tin. I wanted to confide in Dee but decided not to. I was too scared that it would come out into the open. I could still feel the coldness of the ice cream as I entered my house and wondered if it was ever going to melt. I dared not look Mum in the eye, just in case she saw it there. That evening everything was as normal, and also the next day. I was thankful that God heard and had also forgiven me, but the ice cream sitting in me was still frozen and now seemed to be eating me from the inside. I wondered if it would ever digest.

A couple of days later I was sitting down on the floor in the living room with my back up against Mum's chair. I was building Lego houses with Dee, whilst Chris played nearby by himself with a pack of cards. Dad came in and sat down in his armchair with a cup of tea and, soon after, Mum came in from the kitchen and sat down in her chair. Mum put her hand on my head and began gently stroking my hair. I felt the love from her hand gently seeping into me through the crown of my head and I felt tears well up in my eyes. Mum said, "I am so blessed to have such wonderful children, I really am so thankful." Dee asked, "Why Mum?" Mum replied, "My friend told me that a friend of hers had one of her children steal money from her purse, and she was so upset. I told her, 'Oh, how sad. I know my kids would never do a thing like that'".

I felt the earth move from under me and I wanted it to gobble me up whole, just like I'd gobbled up the ice cream, which was now melting under the warmth of Mum's hand. I got up from the floor and ran upstairs to the bedroom, flung my body onto the bed, and cried into my pillow so nobody could hear me. I asked God not to let my Mum know what I'd done, and I promised to never do it again, and I never did. Weeks later, unable to bare the distance my thoughts were creating between us, I confided in Mum. But, of course, Mum already knew; she had to account for every penny. Instead of punishing me the so-called normal way, she brought me back to who she knew I was, nurturing the inner light I was born with. She trusted, loved and expected more of me and, in that expectation, I had to become more.

Whilst in my bedroom, with my face stuffed into the pillow, I remember hearing a faint scream. 'Who made that sound?' I looked around but I was all alone; there was nobody there. As the tears began to subside and the sound slowly began to melt away, I began to realise that it didn't come from outside of me, it came from somewhere deep within. It was the guilt I could hear. It was My Scream.

My Scream reflections

In my wanting of the ice cream, I made up stories in my mind, trying to justify the theft, but my inner light knew this wasn't really me and, in me obtaining the ice cream this way, I couldn't enjoy it.

My thoughts about the ice cream, once I had it in my hands, was not a match for its taste, the taste I knew changed with my thoughts about it.

What great parenting for my Mum and Dad to let me find my own way to what was right or wrong for me. If I had received punishment for taking the money, I believe, in the pain of the punishment, the valuable lesson would have been missed.

It was my own thoughts that led to the feelings of disappointment in me that wouldn't let that ice cream melt. They kept it there, teaching me the valuable lesson I needed.

I was so open and in wonder of everything as a child but, as I grew, the world and everything in it became something to be frightened of. I began to see danger everywhere and, as the illuminated eye I'd always looked out of began to close, the openness and wonder that was at the forefront of who I am was being replaced by fearful thoughts and feelings. This leads us on to a story called 'Female Warrior'...

Female Warrior

It was nearing the end of summer. The sun was out, but it had the thermostat down a notch and, if you ventured into the shade, you could feel the undercurrent of colder weather on the horizon, sending a little chill through your body. Up until this day I hadn't had much interaction with wasps. I didn't fear them; they flew around me and I just got out of the way. I watched the kids running around, screaming, chased by the wasp that was circling them, wanting a taste of the sweet stuff they were eating and, the more they screamed, the more the wasp seemed to follow them.

This day, my brother Chris was riding his bike around the grassy area where we lived. Mum asked me and Dee if we wanted our cardigans on, as it was getting a bit chilly. Dee put hers on, but I was far too busy doing cartwheels with my friend to feel the cold creeping in. Chris suddenly started shouting and screaming and moving his body about, almost crashing his bike, and we all stopped to watch him, not knowing what was happening. Chris got off his bike so fast he almost fell off, scrambling and trying to keep his balance. He threw the bike to the ground and ran toward the balcony, still shouting. Dad had already leapt over the balcony and was heading towards him. As they met, Dad asked Chris to calm down so he could find out what was wrong. He then quickly lifted off his T-shirt, revealing a very angry wasp that had somehow managed to get caught in his top and, in its panic at not being able to find an escape, the wasp had stung him several times.

I eyed up the number of stings he'd received and noted the viciousness of his lumps and decided that day to keep away from them, which I did successfully. Sometimes it meant running and dodging, and sometimes it meant giving them the sweet thing they seemed to be after.

It was my first year at secondary school and the very last day before breaking up for the six weeks' holidays. I couldn't wait! Six whole weeks of doing what I wanted to do; what bliss and freedom! This was everything to me. My school life had improved since primary. I was no longer bullied but I was careful with my truth. I observed and listened and, even when it felt safe, I still didn't voice my opinions. I had been tricked in the past into saying stuff, thinking the people I was with were my friends. I found kids to be weird. They would be your friend, then turn on you in a moment, and then everything you said or confided in them became a joke for everyone else.

It seemed clear to me that if you didn't fit in, you stood out for everyone to poke at. So, as I listened and observed their home life, their views and teachings, I saw they were far from the life I led, what I thought about, my beliefs and how I felt. Although I made friends, I never really revealed who I was. I wondered if there were others like me out there in the world, but felt sure that if there were, they didn't to go to school.

So, it was the last day at school before breaking up and I had science. Before entering the class I discovered that our usual teacher was off sick and we had a supply teacher, so my friend and I decided to skip class. After all, the teacher wouldn't know, she didn't even know us. I had never skipped class before, and it was the last lesson before breaking up so we both agreed we would hang around the stairwell in the science block, talking and waiting for freedom to arrive. Sitting on the cold, hard step, talking and laughing, I noticed a bar that ran the length of the stairs from one side of the stairwell to the other. I hadn't noticed it before. I said, "If we jump up and grab onto the bar we can swing," so we tried it and it worked, and was way more fun than sitting on the cold step. We did this for a while, seeing how long we could hold on for, and I always had to hold on the longest for some reason. We then decided to see how far we could swing and jump off and, as I swung, determined to outdo my friend, I went too far out for my feet to safely hit the ground and I came down hard on my arm. The cold, hard surface snapped my bone in two places, the pressure of the bone piercing the layers of my skin as it pushed its way through.

I knew instinctively it was broken; there was no immediate pain, just a weird sensation of disconnection, until a few moments later when my mind informed my body of the disconnection, and my body sent an army of cells rushing to the injury. I felt every one of them as the shock began to fall away and my mind took over. My parents were called, and I went to hospital, where they reconnected the bone and set it in a cast.

My six weeks of freedom was up the creek with no paddle, and this holiday that I had been longing for was not going to be the same. I couldn't swim, run and jump about, or cartwheel. Nothing. How ironic for this to happen on the last day of school and, to make things worse, the cast was going to be taken off the day before I went back to school. After a few painful weeks my arm was healing nicely and itched like crazy. I would slip a pencil into the gap to reach the itch for some relief and, as my arm lost weight, it became smaller and the gap widened.

It was a glorious sunny day and Mum decided to take us to the Lido, an outside swimming pool and, although I couldn't go in fully, I could paddle my feet and observe others enjoying themselves. We were standing in the queue, waiting to go in, when a wasp started buzzing around me. I moved and dodged but it just kept coming, it was relentless. Mum told me to be still, but no way! 'It's not getting in my T-shirt,' I thought. The game went on for ages and I was getting fed up of the chase and, in a moment of anger, I hit it with my towel. The wasp landed on Mum, stung her on her arm then flew away. I couldn't believe it and I was really sorry.

We settled down in a good spot near a tree and Dee and Chris ran off into the water. It was a beautiful day, and everyone was having so much fun. I tried to enjoy the day but kept thinking about all the fun I was missing out on. As I sat there, I thought about the day it happened and wondered why I tried so hard to be the best that day.

Why had I swung so far out just to win a stupid game, and here I was unable to enjoy myself because of it?

As I sat there, I watched Mum busy looking for some drinks in her bag, when a wasp came out of nowhere, landed right by my gap and proceeded to go into the darkness, the space between my arm and the cast. Mum looked up, offering me a drink and could tell instantly something was wrong. My whole face was sweating, and the fear was evident. Mum said, "What on Earth is wrong Frances?" I pointed at my arm, not wanting to speak in case it heard my voice and decided to take revenge. I whispered in a strained and terrified voice, "A wasp has gone down there, it's walking around and going further in." Mum was always so calm in these moments; she never gave us her fear to deal with as well as our own. She moved closer and said, "Just stay still, it will come back out. It's got nowhere to go. The images of my brother's back flooded back, and I felt the restriction of the cast, I felt trapped. I wondered if it was the wasp I'd hit and if it had decided to get me back. I knew, if it stung me, it could just keep stinging and there was nothing anyone could do.

My mind wanted to panic and crush it with the cast against my arm in fear. My breathing became shallow as the fear took over, restricting the flow of energy to my body. Mum remained calm and kept talking to me. I saw her mouth move but couldn't hear her, I couldn't hear anything, the laughter and shrieks of the kids playing, the splashing, it all went away. It was just me and the wasp in the gap where the darkness sat. It became so unbearable; I just gave in, allowing what was going to happen, to happen and, in the stillness of my mind, I began breathing deeply, allowing the flow to reach my body again, and surrendering completely to the moment and what was happening.

It seemed like hours went by before she finally made her appearance. At the entrance of the gap, she stopped for a moment, giving herself a clean and brushing herself off, before flying off into the sunlight. I wanted to cry but couldn't; I want to release the emotion that I knew was inside me, but it didn't want to reveal itself. After a while the feeling of vulnerability was replaced by indignation. The cheek of it! Coming like that, terrifying me, and even stopping to clean herself before flying off. As the relief started to settle in, it was slowly taken over by anger.

Every year after that, in late summer, I would be stung by a wasp in the most unusual places. One went down my polo neck and was flying about in my stomach area. I grabbed it in my hand with the material and it stung me in my heart. Another year she got into my shoe, not a sandal, a shoe. I thought a sharp stone had somehow gotten into my shoe as I walked along but, after taking it off, I discovered a wasp stuck to the side of my foot. I was also stung underneath my armpit as I hung out washing on the line. It only happened once a year, but it was a yearly reminder.

I spoke about it and expected it to happen, and each year it always did. At the time I thought how spiteful and vengeful they were, to sting me every year, for no reason. She had already got revenge for me hitting her that day. She'd not only stung my Mum, but also terrified me. What more did she want? But nature had not sent something to hurt me but rather to get my attention. In my teenage confusion I was slowly forgetting who I was. I was replacing the love that I was and becoming conditioned into anger and fear. I was beginning to forget that nature loved me and was always teaching me. Nature sent messengers, reminding me not to forget who I am and where I really come from.

Wasps are sensitive to ultrasonic vibrations and are affected by high frequency sound. Little did I know I was attracting her to me through my vibration. She wasn't out for revenge; she was a beautiful messenger trying to show me my eyes were closing, and I needed to open them again, before I got caught up in the illusion of the life our mind offers us. I was no longer looking at and connecting with the dancing particles that used to share many happy times with me, and the ego was surfacing.

Her first attempt failed as I waited outside in the queue that day and I dismissed her, brushing her away in anger as a pest. So, she cast her spell in the darkness as she walked along my arm, reminding me of the stillness, the space between the gap that I was slowly closing.

The wasp is a powerful female warrior. An agreement had been made, a collaboration with my heart to keep my real eyes open, preventing the closing of my mind to the truth I know inside.

She returned year after year, until I finally understood and she was no longer needed. The warrior's point had been driven home and I finally 'real-eyesed' she was not my enemy, but a true and loyal friend.

Female Warrior reflections

At this time in my life, I had started puberty and, as you know, it's a time of great confusion. Your body is changing; it's trying to escape into adulthood whilst having a continual internal fight with your inner child.

Observing the result of the wasp in my brother's t-shirt instilled the fear of wasps in me, a fear I didn't have before that incident. This caused my vibration to change and the fear to vibrate out when one was near me. They had never troubled me before then.

I broke my arm on the last day before breaking up for the six weeks' holidays. With my broken arm I had to sit down and observe more as I couldn't join in, giving me time for reflection.

How amazing was it that the wasp travelled down my arm, taking me internally to that place of stillness, and how funny that it came out slowly, and even stopped to clean itself before flying off.

I feel that I broke my arm because my ego was trying to get the better of the bigger part of me. As a child I had laughed at those that got angry when they didn't win a game, as it was only a game, but a part of me was changing, and I felt I had to win to prove to myself and others that I was the best. My soul, my guidance system, was using the things that I cared about to get my attention.

My thoughts about wasps had changed and I began thinking of them as vengeful. My vibration and the frequency I was sending out, brought me a match to that vibration, reaffirming my thoughts and feelings towards them. As soon as I changed what I was doing with my thoughts, my words and my feelings, the wasps left me alone.

The same way I was learning that by changing my perception of the wasps I changed the outcome. I was also learning to use my thoughts in a more positive way. Some would call it 'luck' and, for a while, I did too, but there is no such thing as luck, just an intention and focused desire and a feeling of worthiness. Remaining in your happiness despite what the current situation looks like, can and does bring to you the desire you require, and it's always so much more because the universal forces fill in all the details you forgot you wanted. Let's go to 'Hotel Mexico'…

Hotel Mexico

I am not very good at remembering specific dates and times when experiences and events occurred as, more and more, I have come to live in the present moment. My kitchen clock has no numbers, just the word 'Now' at the points where NESW would be on a compass. It is a reminder that yesterday has gone, tomorrow is not promised, and today is a gift - that's why it's a present; all we have is now.

Of course, I have appointments to keep and like to be on time and for that I have my trusty phone but, really, there is only sunrise and sunset and everything in-between should be a flow with no restrictions, living moment to moment, impulse to impulse, guided by your inner being which is always leading you towards your happiness.

It must have been around 2010 when I had stopped managing the radio station and had a part-time job as a receptionist in a business centre. My friend Lisa, who I met years ago at a women's refuge, had been living with me at my flat when I was re-housed. She was now a happily married woman and working at the local hospital not far from me. Lisa rang me at work one day saying, "Let's go on holiday! Where do you want to go?" Without hesitation I said, "Mexico!" I had no idea why, it just came out of nowhere, and Lisa begun looking for deals.

We were both survivors and in the healing stages of our lives. Lisa and I were certainly a contrast; she was very practical, liked routine. It helped her feel stable. She liked feeling secure and knowing what the next step was. Lisa was very kind and thoughtful and always put others before herself; it sometimes annoyed me and was something we were always discussing. I loved the way she had been determined to get a job at the hospital and she did, and this is where she met her husband. I was more adventurous, carefree and impulsive. I had been caged too long and wanted to feel freedom, and this would annoy her with what she thought was my lack of consideration for myself and sometimes others, but the relationship worked as we balanced each other out. I wanted her to let go and live more, and she wanted me to take more care and rein it in. Having gone through the experiences that led to our meeting in the refuge, we were like the pendulum clock swinging either left or right and needing to find our middle ground, our equilibrium, our balance.

We set off for Cancun, Mexico, and talked about all the things we wanted to do. The one thing we both wanted to do was swim with dolphins. I had heard that we could go out to sea and swim with them in their natural environment and was excited at the thought of wild, free-roaming dolphins swimming with me, but when I thought about it in-depth it evoked a feeling of excited anticipation with a hint of fear, not of the dolphins, but of the sea.

Arriving at our hotel late evening, tired from all the travelling, we were relieved to be escorted to our room on the first floor. The door was opened and my nose, already ahead of my thoughts, breathed in the energy of the room. Then came the thought, "What is that musky smell?" and I felt an uncomfortable vibe. I thought perhaps the newness of different surroundings, the long journey and rain wasn't helping, but we were both thankful to see the beds where we could at last stretch out properly. I noticed there was only one window, and the curtains were closed, so I pulled them open to take in Mexico's beautiful night scenery but, to my horror, found instead what looked like a massive gas canister looking back at me, and a busy road. The canister looked like it belonged on an industrial site and was only about 10 metres away.

I turned to Lisa who was now sitting on her bed, and said, "Come and look at this!" as I relayed the details of what was in front of me. Lisa was tired and tried to make it appear better by saying we wouldn't be in our rooms during the day and would only be using it to sleep in, but what was staring me in the face was not the image of

Mexico that I had held in my mind and heart. For a moment I felt deflated, then a moment later defiant, saying "NO! Mexico offers so much more and tomorrow I will get it sorted."

We awoke to a grey, rainy day, and it matched how I felt when opening the curtains. My feelings about the room hadn't changed in the slightest, despite my now rested and rejuvenated energy. In fact, from the cold light of this dark day I was even more determined to change it. I got myself ready, had a cup of tea and informed Lisa I was heading over to Reception. Lisa voiced concerns about upsetting them and making our stay difficult, but I reassured her as I closed the door behind me.

Setting off for Reception I breathed deeply in through my nose and out through my mouth all the way down the stairs, only pausing to say 'good morning' to passing strangers and cleaners along the way. Slowly descending, I knew there was a room that was perfect for us, and we so deserved it. By the time my foot hit the last step I was full up of power and inspiration. "I know you are with me; send me an angel," I whispered. At the bottom I bumped into a couple. They both had incredible tans and I commented on how great they looked. My skin had not been kissed by the sun in months, making it obvious I was fresh in Mexico. I asked them how their trip was going. They said they had another week to go and, although they loved some aspects of Mexico, they didn't like the food and were unhappy with their room and wouldn't come back to this hotel again. Not allowing their experience to dampen my vision I hoped they enjoyed the rest of the week ahead, quickly said 'goodbye' and headed to Reception.

The man at Reception was very receptive to me but explained there was nothing he could do as the hotel was fully booked. I asked to speak with the manager, hoping that I could at least be notified if something did become available. Whilst I was waiting Lisa appeared and joined me, the manager was called and appeared soon after, and I politely explained the situation in very colourful terms, relaying and showing him the vision I had of Mexico, and what I'd expected. Both manager and receptionist were smiling at me and said they really wished they could help, but it was out of their hands as nobody was due to leave during our stay.

I stayed focused, not allowing my expectation to be dulled by circumstance when the couple I'd met on the stairs, appeared. We smiled and I moved to one side to let them speak. They said they had to leave to go home unexpectedly and had phoned the airline for available flights and, amazingly, had managed to get a flight home that afternoon. After the couple left, we looked at each other and smiled. The manager pointed at me, speaking to the receptionist in his language, and I was told we could look at the room once it had been cleaned.

After waiting a couple of hours, already packed and ready, after all anything was better than this, there was a knock on the door and we were taken up to the 2nd floor. As the door opened I was comforted by the smell of pine disinfectant, the room had a kitchen area, table and chairs, and the whole layout of the room opened up in a welcoming way. I smiled at the colourful, flowery bed covers, such a trademark of many hotels abroad I'd been to, and the room was pleasing – the smell, the layout and the vibe. I ran to the closed large set of curtains, pulling them back eagerly. The scene was beautiful and, OMG, it had a large balcony. Opening up the doors wide, I flooded myself with the salty smell of sea air as my eyes soaked up the beauty of the beach, the sea, the pool. A fishing boat was out at sea. The wooden hut where our meals would be prepared and eaten was sitting in the sea, just above sea level, perched on wooden legs and accessed by a long wooden walkway. Everything was in that one scene.

The man that had shown us the room was smiling at me, eyes alive, intoxicated by the energy that was in the room. He said, "Glad you like," gave me the card and left. I went back out onto the balcony and excitedly called Lisa to look, as a pelican perched on the side of a rock opened up his wings wide and took flight, ready to dive-bomb his dinner. We watched as he aimed, lining up with his desire and dived in to satisfy his hungry belly. The pelican is a sign of resourcefulness, social teamwork, generosity and friendliness.

Looking out of my window in London on a cold rainy day, my image of Mexico had been one of beauty. We didn't have the money to pay for a seaview but I didn't let go of my vision. I could see it, I felt it, and it excited me. No matter what the current circumstance was, by following my impulses and aligning my energy with the creator, I had turned my expectation into a reality, the reality far outweighing the expectation. The image I was offered was so much more than I could ever imagine.

I had become like the pelican, seeing my desire, lining up with it, waiting for the components to come together in divine timing, then diving in to collect the prize. My belly had led me to happiness and was no longer grumbling; it was happy, content and satisfied.

◊ ◊ ◊ ◊

Hotel Mexico reflections

The day Lisa rang me to ask me if I wanted to go away, she asked me where I wanted to go. I didn't know I wanted to go to Mexico but something inside me, did and this led me to the experiences that would not only enrich me, but would expand me in a new way.

I didn't let go of my vision of Mexico and how I saw the beauty of it from our room, despite the circumstances and all the co-operative elements filled in around me as I stayed in the frequency of it.

Some would say what a happy coincidence, but I have learnt not to believe in coincidences. Things don't happen by chance and, once you know this, you become aware that you are bringing things to the forefront so you can see them and know that you are responsible for them being there. If you don't like what you are bringing, you can always change your frequency. That's the diamond, right there.

Going down the stairs I filled myself up with life force energy and asked for assistance from the heavenly realms. I had no way of knowing that the couple I bumped into would play a part in my desire. I wished them a good time with the week they had left.

We had ten days of the beautiful scenery and it was a blessing, as Lisa was ill during the first week and only left the hotel room to eat her meals. The balcony was a blessing as she could stand out there and at least enjoy the view.

At that time, we were unaware that Lisa had an underlying medical condition that was slowly finding its way to the surface and, little by little, over the years, it revealed itself. This took me way back to my childhood and the medical condition that went undiscovered. I'd love to take you with me now to 'Shadow'…

Shadow

Dad had worked at many different jobs throughout his life and was known as a grafter. He could put his hand to anything, and often did. When not at work, he would spend his time being creative. He was always inventing little gadgets and loved taking things apart to find out how they worked, but his real passion was carpentry. He loved working with wood. He told me about all the different types of wood and what they were used for, and would often call me to come and look at the pattern on a piece of wood he'd sanded down, the grain fully exposed, revealing the story of its life and, as I ran my fingers over the smooth surface feeling its softness, texture and strength, my fingers met the grain in a connection of oneness, and it's story came to life in my hands.

I was still in Primary school when Dad's bouts of illness started to get worse. He'd always had them, but with less intensity. He would go from being fun, with lots of energy, to gradually deteriorate day by day until he would be laid up in bed, sometimes for days. Looking back, I believe the days he felt well it was such a relief to him that he milked it for all it was worth, squeezing every last drop and getting the very best out of every moment. We accepted Dad's illness as a part of life. He wouldn't go to the doctors as he didn't trust them after the experience he had coming out of the army. On returning to England all the soldiers were given a medical examination, and my Dad, having contracted malaria whilst in Malaysia, was checked over thoroughly. They had found a shadow on his left lung but had no idea what it was, so he was kept in hospital while they ran tests and tried to figure it out. He remained in hospital for a year and had been given an injection twice a day in his left side. After a year the hospital investigation still hadn't brought anything to light and my Dad, by this time, had become completely fed up with being a guinea pig. He had met Mum just before being admitted to hospital and she'd stayed with him, visiting as often as she could. He had already spent five years in the army, fighting, and was desperate to get on with life, so he discharged himself. That day both him and his shadow left the hospital together. It was to remain by his side for life, never leaving him.

Over the years Mum had lived with and observed his bouts of illness. Mum understood the opinion and concerns he had about the doctors but kept gently chipping away at him and, one day, somehow managed to convince him to see a doctor. From there he was sent to the hospital for further tests. Mum and Dad hoped the tests would finally reveal the cause and hoped it would be the start of his recovery, but all the tests came back negative. The tests revealed nothing and, as they sat there, despondent, in the doctor's office, it was suggested by the doctor that Dad's illness was all in his mind. On their return home Mum and Dad were talking in the kitchen, and I was sitting on the stairs opposite, playing with my farm animals. Dad was furious with the doctors who had asked him if he was making it up so that he didn't have to work. Dad had a very brown, tanned face due to his time in the jungle, but I watched it redden with rage as he said he'd always provided for his family and had worked all his life, how dare they accuse him. Mum listened and understood. She knew him well and knew he wasn't making it up. She knew every now and again something spread its poison inside him and had witnessed it depleting him of his energy. That day Dad vowed he would never go to the doctors again, and he never did.

Dad began finding it hard to keep a job because of the amount of time he was off sick. The doctors refused to provide him with a sick note as they believed nothing was wrong with him, so things started to deteriorate financially. Mum could no longer work as she needed to look after us, and also Dad when he became ill.

Before Dad's illness took hold we used to go for holidays with Dad's sisters and their families. We'd pack up the cars and head off, travelling to and through Spain, like a fleet of gypsy caravans heading off for adventure and excitement. I was too young to remember the images, but the feeling left its imprint in me. Warm feelings appear sometimes when I sit looking out the window of a car. he smell of the leather upholstery tweaks something in my mind, a memory of good times that I can't quite remember, but know are there. This feeling is exaggerated at night as I watch the lights whizz past and hear the noise of the other cars passing by. Feelings of both excitement and comfort rise up in me, as my senses are taken to a time and place by the images and sounds.

It all started to change when Dad could no longer find work and no money was coming in. Back then, to receive financial assistance in any way, you had to prove you were unable to work and, as the doctors could find nothing wrong, they assumed Dad was lying, refusing to provide him with a sick note, so my parents found themselves in a catch 22 situation. We survived on an incentive from the government, a payment given to couples to have more children as the war had depleted the population. One day social workers came round to see us. They told Mum they could only offer her financial support if she left my Dad. Mum was horrified and showed them the door. This only served to infuriate Dad even more. the war, his illness, the doctors and now the welfare had cast a dark shadow over him, and he became convinced there was a vendetta against us as a family. The last straw came when his sisters, wondering why the doctors could find nothing wrong with him, began questioning him. He was extremely offended by their questions and insinuations, and it ended in a full-on argument. This led to even less understanding, with both sides becoming defensive and hurtful. The energy remained in that stagnant place and was left unresolved, with them no longer speaking to each other.

Our electricity supply was cut off as we couldn't pay the bill and candles became our source of light each night when the darkness arrived. I was mesmerised by the flame and spent ages watching it flicker at the slightest movement or breeze. I was always being told to come away from it and to stop going so close, but I loved being close and speaking to it, and I loved the way my breath made it dance in reply. To my dismay we were eventually upgraded and given a paraffin lamp. This became our only source of light along with the warm glow of the coal fire in the living room. I would stare into the fire as Dad put another slice of thick bread on the toasting fork, and watched as the fork hit the coals, igniting them and making them crackle. I would see faces and images amongst the coals as I waited for my turn to eat the hot toasted bread dripping with butter. I've never eaten toast like it since.

Mum became a master budgeter and, to this day, I don't know how she managed. Along the way we had also been given a two-ring gas hob fuelled by a gas bottle. Despite not having much food we had home-cooked meals every day, prepared and cooked with love. We didn't have processed or take-away meals. Those were a luxury only my friends' parents could afford. Whenever I asked for something, like a new toy I'd seen, Mum never refused or said she couldn't afford it. She'd always say, "Yes you can, when my ship comes in." I was happy with this and every now and again would ask, "Has your ship come in yet Mum?", and she'd say, "Not yet love".

I loved my Dad being at home all the time. On his good days he was hands-on with anything we wanted to create. Kids would knock at the door, not always for us, but for Dad, asking for his help with their bikes or broken toys, and he was always willing to help. He'd get his tools and sit outside on the step, showing them what was wrong and how to fix it. There was one boy, in particular, that used to come all the time. He never really played with us but would only ask for Dad; he lived in the flats opposite. I didn't mind him coming until one day I needed help fixing something. Dad let me know he was helping him first, then he'd get to me. I remember following Dad into the kitchen as he went to get some tools. I said, "But you are my Dad and I need you to help me. Why doesn't he ask his own Dad?", and, "Why is he always here"? Dad stopped looking in his toolbox and gave me a side look. I look said I should know better and I did, but I still held onto a slight feeling as I begrudgingly waited for my turn.

It seemed that the other kids Dads were always busy or too tired after work to help, so mine helped fill the gap. Mum was always on hand, ready with a tray of cold drinks, despite not being able to afford it. The parents' first point of call was our house when they wanted to find their child; they were always in and out of our house or congregating around our door. Dad was always ready to help mend their toys and Mum was ready to wipe away the blood from their grazed knees. It was funny how they opted to come to our house instead of going to their own. In the long summer months life wasn't so rough, but in the winter months it was difficult. I woke up in the morning, cold, even though I shared a bed with my sisters. We would wake up, not wanting to move from the spot our bodies had warmed, and would lie there pretending to smoke as we exhaled the frosty air; it really was that cold some days.

I would have to psyche myself up for the walk downstairs, saying 'one, two, three, GO!', as my feet met the cold, hard floor in the bedroom and I tiptoed down the stairs and onto the cold kitchen floor. It was warmer in the kitchen as Mum would have the gas rings on for some heat. We didn't have a TV so, when darkness arrived and the gas lamp was lit, we sat around playing cards, Ludo and Lego. My Dad and brother were very competitive and always wanted to win, but it didn't bother me. I didn't care about winning; it was just a game, but a game I always seemed to win, infuriating them both. I didn't understand why they got so angry. There were no prizes, and what was it they thought they were winning? I found it hilarious how angry they could become over losing a game and, even though I tried to conceal my amusement at winning, they could see it in my eyes, and this only served to aggravate them even more.

I can laugh now but, at the time, growing up in poverty gave me feelings I didn't want to have. I had holes in the bottom of my shoes and Dad would cut out bits of cardboard to fit into the bottom, covering the holes, which worked perfectly until it rained and the cardboard disintegrated. As I walked, I left a little trail of card behind me. I can remember feeling embarrassed as my friends questioned where it was coming from, and I would pretend I didn't know. My clothes were mostly hand-me-downs, given to us from neighbours whose children had outgrown them. I must admit, receiving a big bag of clothes was very exciting and, even now, if someone offers me some clothes, I get that excited feeling again. The kids at school could be cruel and heartless, so I didn't tell them anything about my home life, but the kids at home were different. They shared our Mum and Dad so, if they did have any mean thoughts, they kept them to themselves. I can remember sitting in my friend's house, watching TV. You had to take your shoes off as you entered the house, as they had shag pile carpets. I would bend my toes into the soft, lush carpet, feeling its warmth and comfort. The living room was bright, warm and inviting and we had sandwiches with cheese and pickles on them, and fizzy drinks. As I sat at the table, eating and looking around, I can remember thinking life couldn't get much better than this, and I silently wished I lived here as my thoughts wandered onto the cold, hard floor of home.

As for the young boy, he moved out of the area rather suddenly and we didn't see him again, until I bumped into him one day, about twenty years later. He recognised me instantly, but it took me a moment to recall where and how I knew him. He immediately asked about my parents and, as I talked about them, tears welled up in his eyes. I was taken back by his emotion and didn't understand it, but it all became clear as I listened to him talk. He told me how much he loved my parents and how much they helped him to heal. The attention they had given him as a young boy had helped fill a gap in his heart left by his parents. He went on to tell me that nobody at the time was aware that both his parents had been killed in a car crash when he was young, and his older sister was left to look after him. She was understandably very fearful and didn't like him going outside but, in her love and protectiveness, he was suffocating. Being outside was his only escape. It was the only place he could pretend life was normal. He said his sister would only allow him to go outside to our house as she could see him from the window.

We hugged and cried, and hugged again, and, as we said goodbye and I turned to walk away, I recalled the words I'd spoken that day, all those years ago in the kitchen, and felt the imprint of that begrudging emotion begin to evaporate into tiny particles which flowed straight out from both my heart and my eyes, to be released forever from my body. If it was one thing I was learning, it was to keep my words soft and tender because, one day, I might end up eating them, and that day I did. It was another example to grow and evolve and, as I reflected, I realised that throughout our lives we only have our own personal perspective; we never really know what is going on in other people's minds, hearts and lives. Being kind and loving to others is the most important thing we could possibly do. As I reflected on that episode of my life, I forgave myself for my youthful ignorance and recalled the memories of my family at that time. What a beautiful, kind and loving soul my Mum was, and what a beautiful example of a real woman - loyal, true and honest. Mum never participated in gossip and was never judgemental, being kind and caring to everyone was her true nature. Her heart was pure and she was my Mum. Dad was a freethinker. He was unique, had his own set of rules and principles, and lived by them. I loved his adventurous spirit and his knowledge of things we couldn't see; he knew there were dimensions of reality and had opened himself up to receive insight about them. My big sister Caz was so generous, loving and kindhearted. If she loved you, she loved intensely and deeply. Caz had a hippie soul and wanted peace and love for every living thing on Earth. My little sister Dee was so sensitive and thoughtful, sweet and caring. She found great pleasure in savouring, intensely feeling into whatever she focused on, be it food, a song or a flower. My little brother Chris was so full of energy, he would literally keep running around until he almost passed out from tiredness. He was adventurous, imaginative and creative. He didn't want to grow up, he just wanted to have fun and play. Chris was always willing to play any game I wanted to, and I laughed as I remembered he was always such a bad loser. As I reminisced on my family and their collective qualities that surrounded me growing up, I allowed the happy tears to fall and the flow of liquid love pour out of me, as I thought how blessed I was to have such an incredible family.

Throughout the years Dad's illness slowly crept up on him and, as the shadow of fear travelled up through his body into his mind, it often surfaced, revealing itself through his words, but despite the shadow growing and eventually taking over his mind and body, his spirit, the very essence of him, was always very much alive.

My Dad made his transition at the age of 72. He made us promise not to call a doctor until he had left his body, and the promise was kept. As my brother and I waiting in the stark, bare coroner's office for the results, we were told that prostate cancer was the cause. I asked about the shadow on his lung and the coroner said he found nothing wrong with his lungs, but had found a small puncture wound in his colon on his left side, which meant, every time he ate, a small amount of food escaped into his body, poisoning his bloodstream. He went on to say that this would have made him extremely ill and would have been very painful. I told him about the injections he was given after the war, and he said it was most likely the cause as he had found lots of scar tissue on his left side. The coroner found it incredible that he had managed to live as long as he had. As a family we had witnessed Dad's illness first-hand, and knew it was real, but I found it somehow satisfying to actually have written proof.

I was angry for a while about the shadow that had been cast over our family by unconscious people, and the way our family had been forced to live and, for a while, felt the pain and injustice my Dad and Mum must have felt. If the doctors had believed Dad's illness was all in his head, why not offer him help and assistance? He had been in the war and, despite not having physical scars, this didn't mean scars were not present. I thought about how different life would have been, had the shadow not been found. When I was at school the poverty had made me feel like I didn't belong in the world, that I was somehow less than others, but as I've grown I have learnt that it's not about circumstances, it's not about your environment, it's about your thoughts and perceptions about them. Maybe life would have been different, but would it have been better? Back then I thought differently. I was young, still growing and evolving, but now I would not go back to change my childhood one bit, or trade places with anyone. We may have been poor in monetary terms, but we were rich in the things that really count. The shadow had caused us to become closer as a family, to help others and to value the really important things in life.

My Dad had experienced things he could never bring out into the open. The war had left a shadow underneath his heart that remained with him to the end. The sharpness of the doctor's needle had left its point in him, and his body was poisoned each time he ate. I came to realise that it's Love, and only Love, that has any lasting value. The shadow was not a dark cloud cast over our family, but a beautiful friend and, not despite it but because of it, I learnt that Love is the only thing of any real value.

…Returning home from my friend's house that day, I pushed the door open as it was always on the latch, and was met by the cold, hard floor. The cold, thin tiles stared at me, daring me to take off my shoes. I felt the contrast; it was the complete opposite to where I had just come from. I pushed the living room door open and was met by the laughter and smiles of my family. Caz was reading. Dee and Chris looked up and asked me if I wanted to join them in their game. My Dad was drinking his tea as his roll-up sat, unlit, in the ashtray beside him. The fire was crackling and the welcoming, loving voice of Mum saying, "Do you want a cup of tea, love?" This left an imprint of love so big in my heart that, if I ever had to choose, there would never, ever be any contest between the shag pile and the cold, hard floor.

Shadow reflections

The doctors and medical professionals don't always get it right. Yes, they have learnt a skill, but they can and do make mistakes. They are, after all, only human. Let us never forget that we have an immune system and a body fully equipped to fend off and deal with any disease, and our main cause of dis-ease is our thoughts. How we think and feel about everything plays a massive part in the balance of our bodies.

I didn't remember going on holiday with my family as I was far too young, but subconsciously I did. I felt the energy, the excitement, the adventure of those around me, and knew this was a happy time. Those feelings come back sometimes when the elements are right, when I'm in a car. This is a powerful insight and shows how babies and young children, even at the stage of being seemingly unaware, are soaking up the energy around them.

My fascination with the candles, that I would watch for ages, took me into a meditative state. Watching the flickering of the candle took me out of my thoughts, focusing my attention inward.

My parents always being home not only provided us with a safe place, but also for all the kids in the flats. My parents were substitute parents for a lot of children and the impact this had on them was immense.

Poverty at that time really did give me feelings of inferiority, but only when I was at school. School became a place where I had to pretend to be someone else, as who I really was seemed to be unacceptable.

Other kids had a lot more home comforts than us, but they also had less time and nurturing from their parents, who were probably so busy trying to make the money to keep them in the comforts they liked. It's funny how, as children, you are only really aware of what you don't have, rather than the things you do.

I am not saying we were a perfect family, far from it. We had our fair share of arguments and fights, but the underlying message is that it is all about love and love is the only thing of any real, lasting value.

We never really know at the time just how our words and actions affect others, especially the little ones. It's only when we have grown and become more conscious that we come to know how impactful and powerful we are as carriers of energy, affecting or infecting as we go. I am reminded of this by an event that happened in my Granddad's life, that completely altered his way of thinking and how a set of circumstances (meaningful incidents) helped him grow. I think we should go to 'Feather Duster'...

Feather Duster

During my early childhood years we were lucky enough to live only a 15-minute walk away from my paternal grandparents, and we used to visit them every two weeks or so, depending on how long it took for the dust of the argument to settle down again. It seemed as though Dad always took his duster with him on the visit, brushing it over the dust that was settled there, waiting for him.

My Nan was small in stature, only 4ft something and with a stocky build. What she lacked in size she made up for with her personal power and big personality. Nan was Irish and didn't take any nonsense from anyone, especially not Granddad; she was very feisty and could hold her own in any situation. Nan didn't stand for any misbehaviour in her home and would put us kids in our place in an instant, and we knew it, but her cuddles were the best. She didn't hand them out for the sake of it so, when she hugged me I knew she really meant it; I felt it.

Nan looked tiny next to Granddad, who was over 6ft. He was a mountain of a man, even as he aged. His hands were massive and were wornout-looking, hard and tough from years of heavy work he had done during his life. He had a unique voice. It fascinated and frightened me at the same time. It was naturally loud and very gravelly. It sounded as though the flow of his breath was trying to get past sharp stones in his throat. He managed to sound angry by just saying 'hallo' to you, but when he smiled his eyes lit up; they were warm and loving.

Granddad was very outspoken and opinionated. He seemed to always be getting into heated arguments with people. On our visits he would relay incidents to my Dad as I sat there pretending not to listen. Life, when he was a child, was rough, and you had to be tough to survive. Granddad would say, "Back then, you looked after your own. The neighbourhood was a community. Everyone knew everyone else and they looked out for each other. You could leave your front doors open. Nobody would steal from you."

He had a dislike for policemen, 'coppers', as he called them. He was proud of the way he had caught one at the door, trying to run through his house, chasing after someone from the neighbourhood who had run through and out into the garden, escaping over the wall. He had stopped the policeman at the door, catching his head and leg between it and the wall as it was shut.

I had to pretend not to be listening and would focussing intently on whatever I was playing with at the time, appearing fully engrossed each time they looked around to check. I knew if they got the slightest inclination that I was listening I would have to leave the room. I liked the excitement, the viewpoints and the opinions, and found the stories far more interesting than playing. The big thorn in Dad's side was the pre-judgment and prejudiced attitude my Granddad had towards anyone who came from anywhere other than England and Ireland. My Dad didn't want to hear his opinion on this issue, but it always seemed to surface as the energy of their words unsettled the particles of unresolved dust sitting between them and, with neither of them backing down, the opposing sides of two opinionated people would very regularly escalate into a full-blown argument.

My grandparents lived in a large three-storey terraced house. It was so much bigger than the council flat we lived in. One of my Dad's sisters lived in the top and middle floors, and my grandparents lived at the bottom. They had a large garden which had an outside toilet, the inside walls of which were covered with little images that you used to get on the jam jars. There were lots of different figures; some playing the banjo, some singing and some smiling. Granddad collected them, finding a place for displaying his collection in the toilet. They were called Golliwogs.

I liked looking at them whilst sitting there. I would count how many of each type there were, which helped take my mind off the cobwebs in the corners and wondering where the spiders were.

As I came in from the garden one day, I could hear my Dad and Granddad talking loudly in the sitting room. Their voices were raised, like two swords ready for battle, and I stopped and listened in the hallway as the tone of their voices began to deepen. I could feel the beginning of a heated argument. The battle was about to commence. I opened the door and took myself into the room. It stopped them, and they both turned to look at me as I entered. The energy of the room was dense and solid, not like when Granddad was telling his stories, so I asked my Dad if we could have golliwog stickers in our toilet. I didn't realise what my innocent remark would do, but I found out. That was the day I realised what the images were, what they represented and how angry my Dad could get on the subject, and how ingrained the prejudice and ignorance was in my Granddad. This was one thing they would never agree on.

It was like watching a play on repeat. Nan would come into the room, telling them both to stop. Mum would get our coats, quickly putting them on us and we would get quick pecks on the forehead as we were hurried out of the door and into the street. Dad, unable to contain his frustration, would continue his point of view, telling Mum how ignorant his Dad was. Mum agreed with him but told him it was pointless arguing with him, he would never change his mind. She said, "Can't you just ignore him?" But he couldn't do that.

It seemed Dad's biggest issue was that his Dad had been taught this prejudice from others. It hadn't come from his own experiences. He had not remained open to finding out for himself whether he liked a person for who they were, and not where they come from. Dad was angry that he just went along for the ride on the backs of others in their ignorance. He called him pig-headed and stuck in his ways. We weren't raised to be prejudiced towards anyone and Dad felt very strongly about this. I think his time in the Malaysian jungle taught him so much about others. He told us how special and caring the Malay people were. He had experienced many acts of kindness during his time there, and this must have impacted him deeply. Dad was only a teenager when sent to war, and trying to find himself in the depths of the jungle whilst living in such horrific conditions. Any pre-conceived notions handed down flowed right out of him and was washed away by the monsoon rain.

The children I played with didn't have the same teaching as us; prejudice was taught and openly voiced. I remember a time before I got strong within myself and learnt to fully flex my unique muscles, standing strong in my beliefs. I was playing at the front of my house, on the grass, with a group of friends, when an Indian man walked along by the side of the wall. One of the group shouted out, "Paki," and then the others joined in. I didn't say anything because I knew it wasn't right, but they told me to and kept goading me to say it as we walked along, keeping up with the man. He had not looked around once during this time. I guess he was used to it and knew it was best for him to ignore it.

I knew it was wrong. I could feel it in my stomach, and I felt sick, but forced it out anyway. My word travelled out of my mouth, hitting the man in the back of his head. He stopped and turned around, looking straight at me. Our eyes met and everything stopped in that moment… I saw the disbelief in his eyes, that I had spoken to him that way. I said 'sorry' in my mind and he felt it. His inner light met mine with a knowing that I knew better and he turned and walked away.

I felt the word I had spoken travel right back to me, the letters jumbling and clogging into a messy lump in my throat. I swallowed them whole and felt the bitterness travel down into my stomach, where it sat like a ball of acid. This wasn't me; it wasn't who I was, I thought, as I ran into my house, the tears of bitter disappointment running down my face. I had learnt a valuable lesson that day and knew I had to learn to grow in the direction of who I am. I had to set the example at all costs and not follow it.

My younger sister Dee came into the house one day, asking if she could go to the shop with her friends. Mum asked her which shop, and she replied, "The Paki shop." She listened to my Mum explaining what the word meant and why she shouldn't use it, and she never referred to the shop in that way again. Many words were spoken innocently and unconsciously, without realising the pain and hurt they caused. But we learnt and were thankful for the wisdom and insight.

Each time we visited with Granddad, at some point, Dad would always ask if he had changed the pictures in the toilet, and every time he replied, "NO!" After a while, Dad left his dusting cloth at home and would just head home if the conversation started to head in the direction of the dust.

Years later, my grandparents had gone away for a week in the country and, at the start of their return home Nan became ill. During the train journey, Nan worsened and was finding it hard to walk. Granddad was much older now and, although still tall and sturdy-looking, he no longer had the strength to carry her and the two large bags they had with them. As the train pulled into the station, everyone started hurrying off. Granddad asked for help, but nobody seemed to hear him. He stopped a man and explained the situation and asked him for his help. The man said he was sorry but he was in a rush, and he'd have to ask someone else. Granddad thanked him with a couple of swear words, as the man quickly walked away.

Nan was unresponsive now and he didn't know what to do. He couldn't leave her to go and find someone, and nobody was about. He recalled his younger years and thought back to when he would have carried Minnie, as he called her, and both the bags, needing help from no-one. He sat down next to Nan, one large worn-out hand holding hers and the other covering his face, and he began to cry, something he rarely did. Why had nobody helped him? Why had he chosen to sit in the very last carriage? Why was nobody around? Why did nobody care? Sitting there, tears coming down his face, he surrendered to the moment and asked out loud for help.

Then, just like magic, a man came along, driving one of those carts that transport the mail from the trains to the vans. He stopped and asked Granddad if he was ok. Granddad explained the situation and the man said, "Don't worry, I'll make a space for your lady amongst the letters," and he started distributing them so they could both sit down. They both lifted Nan onto the cart, put the bags on, then, just before Granddad sat down he noticed a feather duster, which he handed to the man. The man smiled. "It's for my letters, they get very dusty," he said, and then started up the cart.

As they rode along, Granddad explained how frustrated and helpless he had felt when nobody had stopped to help them. He also hoped the man wouldn't get into any trouble for putting them on the cart. The man smiled and said he could lose his job, but he couldn't drive past leaving him there, it wasn't right. "We have to look after each other," he said. Granddad couldn't thank him enough and hoped his kindness wouldn't cost him his job. As they reached the end, the man waved at a policeman standing at the entrance of the station and he came over. He explained the situation and the policeman told them not to worry, he would get help. He sent for an ambulance and both the man and policeman waited and chatted with Granddad until it arrived. Safely in the ambulance, Granddad shook the policeman's hand, saying goodbye to the copper. He turned and hugged the man that helped him, gave him his address, and told him he would speak for him if he got into trouble. The man smiled and said, "Thank you, but I have a feeling it will be ok."

Nan recovered quickly. They weren't sure what it was or what had caused it. Granddad retold that story to everyone and anyone that would listen; he spoke proudly about the only man that came to his rescue. He painted over the images in the toilet and, if anyone spoke negatively about a person of colour, he would say in his gravel tone, "Fix yer mouth in my company or I'll fix it for ya".

My Dad had spent many years trying to sweep away the dust of ignorance and didn't succeed, but one act of kindness had reached in, brushing it away softly with his feather duster, clearing the way for a new, fresh perspective, and an embracing of those he had been taught to fear.

The man that rushed by, too busy to help, was white and Granddad's words went unheard. The man, the angel that had come to his rescue, was black and had not only heard them, but felt his words, and had found the space he needed between the letters.

Feather Duster reflections

I loved recalling this time with my Granddad and, on reflection, how my experiences back then moulded and shaped my personality. I want to share, not just my story, but the lessons and teachings that came from them in the hope that something in them resonates with you and your life.

My Dad spent many years trying to force his Dad to change his opinion, but it seemed, the more he forced it, the more defensive his Dad became.

Children are always listening, no matter what they are doing, even if it seems as though they are fully engrossed in their toys. They are still picking up the energy, the frequencies, the images and sounds around them, and this all plays a part in their growth.

Sometimes the gentle approach of kindness comes in and completely alters an attitude or outlook. It's not always the forced opinion of others that changes a person, but the kindness, the love, compassion and understanding another, that will always be a powerful force for change.

Take a closer look at your opinions, your attitudes and check to make sure they come from your own heart and mind, and they are not just handed down opinions. Remember, we are raised and conditioned from birth by others. Check that you are not stereotyping or buying into a pre-conceived notion of others. Where do your beliefs come from? Are they from your experiences?

We all need to sit in our truth; we feel it in our gut when we have gone against our true essence, and this is our true guidance system. It takes courage and confidence to stand for something you believe is right, no matter what. You have this courage inside you; you have everything you need inside you. Life is bringing you opportunities to go deep inside and bring it out. Are you being your authentic self? Are you really showing your uniqueness, even if it means being unpopular? Are you setting the example of the person you want to be, and not just following along with others for an easier life?

We have all, at some time in our lives, worn a mask or a uniform to blend in, or pretend that we are something that others will approve of, but we need to take them off and ground ourselves in our uniqueness. Underneath, we are all sparks of divine light in human form. Our colour, our religions, our gender, our uniforms, make no difference as we all want and deserve love, understanding, compassion, peace, happiness and freedom. At some point we all ache to fill the void, to seek that connection and to find the deeper meaning of life. When the colour of a man's skin no longer matters and the uniform is off, we at last understand we are all one. Are you ready to remove your mask and reveal all that you are underneath?

It's good to try to show people your perspective if you see they are holding onto beliefs that you feel are not valid and come from a place of fear, as sometimes all they need is another perspective, but if you find you have to keep trying to convince them, or you end up in confrontations and arguments over who's opinion is the right one, then it's best to get out of the way and allow the universal energy to give them the experiences needed for their growth.

There are positive forces, energy in the form of angels that can assist us and are ready to, but you have to remember to ask. Free will is given to us at birth. We have to make our choices and every decision is ours to make. It is our birthright, and they cannot interfere unless we ask them to.

I have found the best way to help someone awaken from a conditioned mindset is to first let them know your truth. Do not argue - there is no point. Just speak your truth calmly and clearly, then allow the seeds to find their root. I find it best to ask out loud for the person's awakening and visualise them as the light being they really are' and then be satisfied in the knowledge that the lesson will come at the right time and will be received in a way so that is so much more powerful than anything I could try to make them see, and as the experience has been divinely orchestrated, it will be completely transformational.

In the kind space the mailman made between the letters, is where my Granddad found his true nature.

I want to ask a question to all those that feel they are completely free from prejudice. Ponder on it, process it, and answer it honestly. If a spaceship landed on Earth and an unusual-looking being stepped out, saying he had come in peace, would you embrace him and share knowledge with him, or would you meet him with fear?

I found it very inspiring to watch the dramatic change of Granddad's lifetime belief completely turnaround. It gave me great hope for the future of mankind. My journey has been full of meaningful incidences, some would call them 'coincidences', but you know I don't believe that. Let's journey now to my 'Angel's Kiss'...

Angel's Kiss

Something I said, or didn't say, did or should have done, who knows, and it really was irrelevant, as a reason could always be found. He had struck me on the left side of my face, accusing me of talking back in a tone and manner he didn't like. It was the same side where he had given me a hairline fracture in my jaw months ago and, although the strike hadn't caused much damage, it had created a toothache, one I couldn't ignore.

I had a doctor's appointment booked for the morning before the dentist, as I had missed a period; I already suspected but needed confirmation that I was in the early stages of pregnancy. I had already been blessed with two beautiful daughters, so completely different in personalities and, although still young and growing, I could already see an array of gifts they possessed inside of them. I loved them with all my heart and loved the closeness, the love and feeling of connection we shared.

My eldest, Maxine, was a complete blessing to my life from the moment she was born. Max showed herself to be an incredible being of light. She was open, kind and always full of laughter. She drew you in with her warmth and friendliness. It was impossible for all who met her not to love her, as she loved unconditionally and without judgment. She was always laughing and instinctively knew how to make others laugh. Max had a beautiful gift of being able to look right into the best, the realest part of you, slowly, bit by bit, tugging on it, pulling on it until, eventually, bringing it out into the light for you to see it too. I had seen her do it many times, and with people who did not have much of a light showing, those that hid it behind the coldness and harshness of their lives.

My second daughter, Lydia, arrived into the world just at the right time, enhancing my life to the fullest. Lydia was an amazing being of light, so deep and mysterious, very wilful and strong, but also ultra-soft and sensitive to vibrations, and she picked them up accurately and quickly. There was no coaxing her into liking someone if she didn't, no matter who they were. Lydia stayed very close to me at all times and never even stayed at family members' houses without me. Lydia seemed to unnerve people she didn't know and would stare deeply at them, as if searching the very depths of their souls, sensing the different facades and layers of protection they wrapped themselves in. Lydia had a beautiful gift of intuitively knowing when someone wasn't being who they really were, and they felt that knowing when she looked at them.

My doctor confirmed that I was expecting, and my first thought was, 'Another incredible life on the way!!', followed by the second, 'Why on Earth am I bringing another baby into my life?' Things had changed dramatically since first being with him, and it was steadily getting worse. I was losing every battle I had with him to keep him away from the drink and drugs that were helping him to lose both his mind and his heart. Looking back, I had always wanted and expected an extraordinary kind of love. I didn't want 'normal', 'marry and have kids', 'home and work'. I wanted more. I wanted excitement, exhilaration; I wanted to know I was alive in every sense of the word. I wanted a man like Spartacus, someone different from the crowd, someone that stood for something and one that loved me beyond the love most know. I hadn't really liked him when I first met him, but he chased me a bit and when we finally got together and I got to know him, I found him exciting. It was our first argument that cemented it. I had jumped on a bus heading towards my Mum's, putting an end to the argument we were having. I wasn't listening to him calling me as I jumped on the bus and sat down. The bus had only gone a few stops when the driver suddenly pulled up, and shouted, "Idiot," as we all tumbled forwards, nearly meeting each other in the middle of the walkway. The bus door opened, and he got on, headed towards me, told me he was sorry, took my hand and pulled me off the bus. He had pulled in front of the bus with his car to get me. I was young and impressionable and must have thought this was the extraordinary love I was looking for… but it wasn't, it was in disguise. It was really possession and control.

Why continue to stay with him now; why put up with the abuse? Why not just leave or get him out? But it really wasn't that simple. He was very well known and feared. I couldn't go anywhere without him knowing. He seemed to know everyone and had himself a reputation which made a lot of people scared of him, and rightly so. I had witnessed events that planted seeds of fear in me and, over the years, those fears had taken root, gaining a stronghold, and the seed sitting there surrounded by darkness couldn't seem to break open to search for the light. He kept that fear fed and watered regularly, topping it up, just in case I forgot. He was a master manipulator and had mastered skills in using his words, facial expressions and his darkest level vibrations to cause reactions, homing in on a weakness or vulnerability, using it to his advantage to get the result he wanted. We had already had the discussion about what would happen if I ever left him. He let me know it wouldn't take him long to find me, he had eyes everywhere, and I knew that was the truth. He let me know how angry he would be to have to search for something that was already his. He knew the children would have to go to school at some point, so he could easily trace me. He didn't directly threaten but said, if all else failed, he knew where my parents lived and if I left him, he'd have nothing to lose. I felt trapped and nobody could help me.

I had tried communicating my feelings to him in the early years, but it didn't work. I tried fighting back but it was useless. He was a boxer, martial arts and street fighter, and I wasn't prepared to take it to another level. I was no match for the pain and anger he had inside and, despite my efforts, I couldn't dissolve or fight that. Although I knew most arguments were unjust and wrong, the amount of worry and anxiety they caused my girls wasn't worth me being right so, little by little, I gave up my truth and kept quiet, trying to keep the peace and limit the damage. I went inwards, becoming a master observer and a feeler of energy.

Sitting in the dentist chair, thoughts of wanting the baby so much were running around in my mind, being chased by thoughts of my home life and wondering if it was even fair to the baby. My thoughts played tag for a while until, finally tired out from all the chasing, my want for this new life became the clear winner and I settled down and recalled the feelings I had for my girls when they were babies, the smell of their new skin and how soft they felt. Their first smiles, giggles and laughter. I recalled how their tiny hands wrapped around my finger tightly as we looked at each other, creating the sacred bond. I remembered the feeling it gave me deep down in my soul; it was a connection to something far greater. It was pure; it was beyond the realms of this physical world. I didn't want to name it, as if giving it a label would take away its value. I placed my hands on my stomach and felt it again. In that moment my heart burst open. As I held the feeling in my hands it was as though the curtains were suddenly drawn in a darkened room, allowing the light to stream in so I could see clearly. The feeling I had with each of my babies was real love, a powerful love. It was so pure, so unconditional and it had no ending. In that moment I realised it was the love my creator feels for me. The creator was in me, and I was in it. Tears streamed down my face and I allowed them to flow freely.

I was rudely brought back by the dentist staring down at me. He offered me a tissue and told me not to worry, reassuring and promising to be especially careful with me. I laughed inwardly as he was so far off the mark, as the fear of the dentist was not present at that time. I was in ecstasy and my tears, if bottled, would be worth millions. I had to have a filling at the back as my tooth was cracked. It had already been prepared and the dentist was ready to go in for the kill. I wished I had some music to listen to and focus on, instead of listening to the sound of the drill. I prepared myself mentally for both the pulsating and high-pitched sounds that would be sending its frequencies through my entire body. I really hated going to the dentist; I'd lost trust in them a long time ago. As a child, my dentist had ruined my experience and my teeth. I had broken my front tooth in half, sliding down the sloped bit in the bath, the bit you rest your back against. I loved sitting on the little ledge and sliding into the water. It was great fun, but Mum wasn't amused with half the bath water ending up on the floor.

I had been sliding down this particular day when my big sister Caz came into the bathroom just as I was perched, ready to go again. Mum had sent her up to tell me to stop and she pointed out all the bath water that was on the floor. Caz told me I was going to hurt myself if I carried on, but I was ready and prepared to slide. I told her, "Just once more," and, as I slid down the water turned me over and I hit my mouth against the bath, breaking my tooth.

I had never felt pain like it before. For the next few years Mr Morcus became responsible for my dental work. I felt every filling, every press of the drill, as it bored down into the depths of me, causing panic and dread every time I had to attend. Years later I learnt Mr Morcus had been struck off as a dentist and was unable to continue his practice. Too many people had complained and he was found to be incompetent. But the damage had already been done. The drill had infiltrated me, and the pain remained in my mind and body and could be recalled anytime I thought of that damn drill. The dentist I was now seeing knew about my experiences and was pleasantly reassuring and extra careful with me. The job was done, the filling sorted, and I didn't feel a thing. I couldn't move my mouth but that was to be expected. He had felt sorry, seeing me crying, so had dosed me up properly. It would wear off in a couple of hours he said, but it never did. The whole evening passed, and my mouth had not improved and seemed to be getting worse. I couldn't smile or close my left eye; the whole left side of my face was affected.

The next day both the dentist and the doctor told me it was Bell's Palsy, the actual cause was unknown. It's the result of swelling and inflammation of the nerve that controls the muscles on one side of your face, and it can come on suddenly, I was told. Had it been caused by the dental work or the strike I received? Perhaps it was a bit of both. Nobody knew for sure, but it was awful. I found it hard to drink, eat or smile properly, and felt externally disfigured. It was a very slow recovery, and at that time, doctors didn't know much about it, so could offer no real solution. I had one electrode treatment, where small electric shocks were given to parts of my face to try to stimulate the muscle, but it didn't seem to do anything. So here I was, one side of my face not working, and my belly growing. Apart from my face, things had eased up a bit at home. He held his hands out to carry the responsibility of maybe causing it and, to be honest, I allowed him hold it, not offering him any excuses or accusing him either way. When he upset me, I'd take myself somewhere quiet, hold my belly with both hands, talking softly to the little spirit growing inside and telling him or her, "Not to worry, Mum's here, I love you," just as I'd done with my girls.

My scan was due and, upset from yet another argument, I went to my scan by myself. I was so angry and frustrated at always having to bite my tongue to maintain peace and preventing the escalation of violence that would follow. My anger quickly faded away as I saw the image of my baby boy on the screen, heart pumping and kicking around. He was certainly a lively one.

I already had two beautiful girls and now I was having a boy, what a blessing. I felt elated and a smile erupted on the right side of my face, my left side no longer able to keep it contained. My face slowly improved during my pregnancy. I was able to smile, although it was lop-sided, and each time I did, my left eye would close automatically, but it did resemble a smile. When my son was born the feeling of love I had was immense, and as I held him in my arms, my face seemed to improve straight away, my distorted face no longer able to contain my happiness. Aron was born tongue-tied. The tongue and the floor of his mouth had fused together when he was growing in the womb. I was curious as to what caused it as the doctors couldn't give me a reason. I asked the doctor if my feelings of not being able to speak my truth had caused it, but the doctor looked at me confused, dismissing the possibility and went on to give me a medically scientific explanation that still didn't make it any clearer.

Then I noticed that the tie was in the shape of a heart, and I knew instantly and intuitively that the connection was real.

Aron was a beautiful smiley baby; he was always happy and had a smile at the ready, always. He never cried, ever, he just made a little sound, and as soon as you looked at him, he smiled. When he was upstairs in his cot and woke up, he wouldn't cry, he would just rock his cot against the wall, making it bang until I came up, and as soon as I opened the door he would be looking and waiting to give me one of his beautiful smiles. He was loved by everyone that met him and his sisters adored him.

Aron was also born with a birthmark, and I believe it was no coincidence that it was on the left side of his forehead, a lucky omen with the special meaning of a life purpose and destiny. It is now known that a foetus in the womb donates stem cells to the mother helping her heart to heal; on his forehead was the mark of thanks and appreciation from the heavenly realms for the cells and love exchanged. It is the sign of protection… the mark left behind by an angel's kiss.

Angel's Kiss reflections

As I look back, I realise I was not very good at being told what to do as a child and sometimes didn't listen in time to prevent something unwanted from happening.

When you are young you are impressionable, and what appears to be something you desire, you can later find out was not what you thought it was. As you grow you learn to be more discerning, as you tap into that bigger part of you, using your intuition and inner guidance instead of being impressed by outward appearance.

By going inwards and becoming an observer I learnt how to read energy and could often see things happening way before they had started, and I used this, not only in situations that caused me to need a heightened awareness, but in everyday life. I watched people talk, how they acted and could see the energy in their words and actions.

I don't believe in coincidences, as in something happening by chance. I believe in the connection of co-operative elements coming together and blending into a physical form. The connection between me feeling stifled at not being able to express my feelings through words, and my son being born tongue-tied, was no coincidence. Neither was the connection between the left-hand side of my face and my son's birthmark on his left side of his forehead.

I learnt how the fear of what could happen can stop you from making the steps you need to take for your own safety and sanity. Imagination can be a wonderful thing, but when it is fuelled by fear it can be horrendous.

Fear can be crippling, preventing you from moving and becoming more. It can consume you, taking over completely, but if you push through the fear, getting into the driving seat of your mind, you can get to a place of knowing the power you really are. Come, let's go to the caves in Mexico to the one called 'Dos Ojos'…

Dos Ojos

My days in Mexico were fast becoming more than great days out and more like spiritual encounters. I was fully engrossed in soaking up and absorbing the energy from every experience.

Today we were visiting the Ancient Mayan ruins and would be snorkelling in the underground caverns, cenotes as they were called, that were situated around them. There had been lots to choose from, Mexico had so many but, whilst looking at our choices, we were drawn to the one called Dos Ojos, meaning 'two eyes'. We would be heading to Tulum on the northern peninsula, where the lakes and streams had provided the water supply to the ancient Mayan people long ago. We were informed that the cenotes we were visiting today were used to offer human sacrifices long ago and both Lisa and I looked at each other briefly before I turned my attention inwards and thought of the people, their families and the fear they must have felt being offered up as a sacrifice.

The sun was gloriously warm, even this early in the day and, as I sat down in the window seat of the coach and looked out of the window, the sun found my eyes and I had to squint. Although uncomfortable, I was not willing to look away from the beauty that surrounded me. As we set off, I could feel it was going to be a really beautiful day. It had an exciting vibe about it, but I noticed, in the distance, a dark raincloud approaching from the north. It was huge and menacing and it was catching up with us, like a dark shadow creeping up on the unsuspecting with a determination to remove any chance of any light or joy. It wasn't long before the dark cloud caught up, engulfing us, completely separating us from the sun, its warmth and the light it radiated, surrounding us on all sides in a dark grey light. The rain was furious for some reason, and came down hard and fast, hitting the windows in fits of anger. Moments later the sun gently peeked through a slight gap in the dark cloud and, seizing its opportunity, burst its way back through to take centre stage again. The sun was not going to be outdone today, I thought, as the light, the warmth and the sense of joy returned to my window seat.

I was thinking how fast life can change; in the blink of an eye everything can change; we are only ever living from moment to moment, when my thoughts were interrupted by Lisa asking me if I wanted a drink. I took a drink and sat chatting to her for a while, but soon my thoughts took over. I was glad I was a good swimmer; Mum had taken us to a swimming club twice a week, ensuring we were more than confident in the water, and I had been thankful for that several times in my life. I had never snorkelled before and was looking forward to the new experience.

On arrival we were given a run down on what to expect and what the caves were all about. The cenotes, as they were called, occur when a cave collapses under water, causing sinkholes. These underwater channels and passageways can go on for miles and provide an exquisite window into a completely different world. Before entering the water, we had to shower to remove any sunscreen, perfumes or ointments from our skin, as it pollutes the water, killing the fish and marine life.

The entrance to the cave was breathtaking. Stalactites hung down from the cave roof and the roots of a tree hung down through the top, exposing its vulnerability as the tree desperately sought stability. the cave had no choice but to leave it hanging there as it crumbled. Dos Ojos was rightly named, as the entrance did look like it had two eyes. I was glad we booked the earlier trip as, looking around, there were not many of us in the snorkelling group. There was one group of divers, and the other, snorkelers. The divers would be entering the left eye and needed a guide with them at all times, but we could independently experience the right cave, travelling at our own pace. We were told that, as we travelled along the cavern passageways, we would come to clearings where we could get out, take a rest and lifeguards would be situated at every clearing.

The water was crystal clear and was lit up from beneath the water. There were schools of fish swimming below and I felt a hint of fear, a feeling of the unknown surfaced in me as my thoughts of the sea and everything in it waved through and over me, so I took my attention away and looked up and around at the rock formations, hand-crafted and sculptured lovingly by nature's own hands. I could see faces, bodies and eyes peering back at me, and was both mesmerised and frightened at the same time. As I got in, the water felt both warm and cold at the same time. It was the blend of salt water and fresh water flowing through together, creating a layer, I was told. It felt so strange, like being in two worlds at the same time, a warm world on top and colder one below, although together, they remained separate, not mixing or uniting.

As we swam off, taking the right eye, we lost sight of the others who seemed to be in a hurry to get to their destination. We swam along leisurely, taking in the wonder and incredible surroundings. Looking below me in the water I could see holes in the side of the caverns and wondered what lived inside. We had been informed that eels, fish and bats were present, but nothing we need to fear. We had to remember to keep away from the sides of the cave as the rock formations often had sharp edges, so we were careful to stay in the middle, taking in and making the most of every moment of this amazing place. I swam alongside the fish and noticed things moving beneath me that I couldn't make out. The fear was coming and going as the beauty and the unknown blended, but didn't mix.

I was in awe of its creation and in love with its creator as I travelled along the route, stopping along the way at the clearings for a rest and, as promised, lifeguards were always present. After stopping at one of the clearings we decided to call it a day at the next one, as we had been in the water for hours. I noticed there were two passageways, the larger one was well lit and was inviting, and the other was dark and ominous. Lisa and I got into the water and looked along the dark one. We could just see a light at the end, which seemed a long way off and had a very eerie feel to it. The lifeguards asked if we wanted to try the dark passageway or remain on the lit route. Not many tried it, we were told. We discussed it for a while. We could either take the lit route, the one that invited us to play, or we could challenge ourselves by taking the route that offered us the chance to control our thoughts and surpass our fears. It was decided that we would enter the route less travelled, and the lifeguards clapped for us, before radioing ahead to the next set of guards.

As we began to swim through, I turned to Lisa and told her to keep her head above water. I had mistakenly looked down and almost lost all breath as I saw nothing but darkness beneath me. As we swam further along, we were engulfed on all sides by darkness. We spoke to each other about the light ahead and how good it's going to feel when we reached it, desperately trying to keep the darkness from taking over. I couldn't look down as it terrified me and, as my eyes got accustomed to the dark, I looked up and noticed something moving on the roof of the cavern. I think it was a bat. Well, I hoped it was, as a cold shiver seeped through my body. I decided not to mention it to Lisa; it served no purpose other than to add to the fear and decided to focus all my attention on the light, so far away.

We acknowledged the halfway point with the sudden realisation there was still a way to go and decided to swim a little faster. Just then I felt something brush past my leg and an intense fear rose up in me. Lisa felt it brush past her too and the overwhelming fear travelled up from the pit of our stomachs and exploded as the fear was voiced, causing a tsunami of echoes that bellowed back at us from the menacing faces of the rock formations. The fear turned into panic and we both lost control of our emotions, the images of sharks and unknown monsters beneath the sea came vividly rushing back from the stored crevices and caverns of my mind. Every frame, image and clip came out of nowhere to find me, to be with me in this moment of darkness. Still so far to go, I couldn't breathe and knew I had to gain control as the flow of life force energy was being cut off. I couldn't think clearly with these images and fear taking me over.

I had been here before, I remembered. I stopped swimming and panicking and was now treading water. I took hold of Lisa and started breathing deeply and told her to do the same. We began treading water and looking at each other; we needed to stay in control. I said that we had been through the caves when they were lit. We had to remember what they looked like, we had to remember the beauty and how it really looked. It was the same water, the same fish, but with the light off. Lisa agreed and we continued to talk, encouraging each other as we swam; we took back our control and the light got nearer and nearer.

As we reached the end of the darkness we were exhumed by light and surprised to see a few people with the lifeguards, clapping and cheering for us. We had freed our fears in the dark tunnel and shone a light in the dark thoughts of our minds. We later learnt that the cenotes are sacred to the Mayan people. The sinkholes represented a passage to the underworld, and they believed that Xibalba, Place of Fear, was a place where the spirit of the Gods lived and roamed free.

We had been taken to the place of fear and had swum with the spirit of the thoughts that roamed there. They had touched us, feeding and controlling our emotions for a while, but the fear is not a place, the fear is in your mind. In that dark tunnel is where you find that the light is not somewhere you have to get to, because the light at the end of the tunnel is not an illusion… the dark tunnel is.

Dos Ojos Reflections

When we were looking at the different cenotes in Mexico, we were drawn to that particular one. Our inner light knew that if we chose the dark tunnel it would give us the experience that we needed to bring to the surface anything that needed to be released, showing and empowering us, and helping us to evolve.

Nature is so magnificent; the tree that was hanging in the front of the cave was still alive. It had maintained its hold and was growing, despite the cave crumbling. Although the roots were exposed and vulnerable, it was not giving up and its power was in its will to live.

The beautiful contrast was there all day long - the rain, the water, and the dark. If we didn't have the dark, how would we know to choose light? We have free will to choose whatever tunnel we want and to see things however we want. It's all a matter of perspective. Just like we can change our minds, our thoughts can also change our lives.

We could have chosen the easy tunnel, the one that was lit up, so we could continue just seeing all the wonders and beauty it held, giving us a continual lovely experience in the cave, but we would have missed out on the extraordinary bonus of living an experience that brought us deeper clarity and confirmation of just how powerful our thoughts and feelings really are.

The dark cave was exactly the same as the one that was lit up but, because it was dark and we couldn't see much, our other senses were heightened. Our minds released all the images we'd ever seen on things that can appear in the dark. The reality was, it was the same as the beautiful tunnel, but with the light off. This is something to remember in those times of darkness.

Being told about the cenotes and the sacrifices that took place had planted a seed of fear before we arrived, and this was fed by the rock formations with its grimacing faces and images, adding to the fear, so it grew and grew.

The power of gaining control of your mind, allowing the bigger part of you, your true essence, to steer the mind in the way it wants to go, stops it from running wild with the information it has collected during its lifetime. I have found that breathing deeply is essential in staying in control and allowing the flow of life force energy to reach every part of my body.

This amazing experience in the caves of Mexico assisted me in releasing the fear I thought I'd gotten rid of. I thought I was completely free, but it's a continuous journey of releasing and the choosing of thoughts of a higher nature. I came to understand that fear comes at you in many different ways, and it's something that has to be overcome constantly. I also realised my soul was making sure it came in at all angles so I could learn to master and control the thoughts that fed its hungry belly, so we could eventually be free. My next and last experience is called 'Free from Fear'...

Free from Fear

Here I was, standing just 6ft away from him in the bedroom, while he sat at the head of the bed in a slouching manner. His eyes were cold and the intent focus of his stare sent a shiver of ice along my spine as I desperately searched for signs of light in his dark eyes, but could find none. I knew there was light, I had seen it, felt it and had laughed and joked with it, but now his mind was so taken over by the drink and drugs he had consumed, they were now consuming him, allowing the pain he refused to let go of, escape and find a way up to the surface.

I searched for him again with my voice, hoping my words would find a way in to water down and dilute the growing fire raging inside him, but they only fuelled him as he piled them on, using them as logs to add to his fire. Standing here in my nightdress I felt vulnerable and cold, and could feel myself shaking from the inside. I took another deep breath in as my averted eyes fell again on the shotgun aimed at my stomach. I looked straight at him, trying to remain strong; I knew I could show no signs of weakness as this would only feed his need for power. Would he pull the trigger? Yes, in this state he would. It wasn't just a fear or an illusion my mind had made up. He had hurt me badly before so the threat was very real. Thoughts were running around in my head, looking for a way out, an escape from the situation they found myself in. Twenty minutes ago I had been tucked up in bed, sound asleep. I knew I hadn't given him a reason. He didn't need one. His mind made up so many stories, he could make any one of them a reason. The questions in my mind picked up pace. Should I try to make a run for it? In his intoxicated state, would I be able to outrun him? But the different scenarios of what could happen kept me there. If I ran, my children were only in the room down the hallway and, in his frustration to get me, he might pull the trigger and the bullet could go through the paper-thin walls, or they might come out of the room. Anything could happen, and accidents do. Seeing no way out, I chose to just stand there and hope that it worked itself out.

It didn't matter what I said or how I said it, how I acted, or didn't. My very presence irritated the life out of him and triggered every hateful, vengeful thought and feeling he could find in the stored crevices of his mind. I had learnt to read the energy and adapt myself, so I was not pushing up against the dark energy that was around me. I had learnt to control my mind with deep breathing, going inward instead of becoming totally absorbed and lost in the energy. I had to stay in control, my survival depended on it.

I recalled the time he had told me he would always be able to tell if I was lying. He said, "If I ask you a question and put my hand on your heart, if your heart is beating fast, you are lying." I had argued the point with him as being unfair, telling him fear and anxiety would give the same result, but he didn't listen and I received the back of his hand as a reply. After that, on his bad days, he would sometimes ring me, upset about something, and inform me he was coming home to question me, letting me know what he would do if I was lying. The anticipation of what was to come sent me into panic mode. All the hairs on my body rose up like antennas, ready to signal his approach. My breath would become shallow, restricting the flow of life force energy going to my heart, as it beat in disharmony with the thoughts of what was to come. I knew I had to find a way to stop this, and I thought that surely if my heart wasn't beating fast, then I wasn't lying. I practised and practised, choosing my thoughts carefully and inhaling and exhaling deeply, allowing the flow to expand, not just my lungs, but also my mind. The next time it happened I found myself in a place of complete calm, and even my hairs no longer notified me of his presence. The look he gave me said it all, and I took a snapshot of the disbelief on his face so I could treasure it. That day I found great satisfaction and power in my peace.

As I breathed deeply, it was as if he could see I was trying to gain control, and this seemed to madden him. It was like I had poked the fire hard with a stick, making it flare up, crackle and spit in defence. He finally spoke, asking me if I knew what a gun like this would do to my stomach if he shot me, especially at close range. I didn't answer and he shouted, "DO YOU!" I replied, "No." He told me it would leave a gaping hole so big, he could look through me and I would take a long time to die. The thought sent a chill through my already cold body as the fear ran blindly through my bloodstream. My heart was sent into panic mode as I tried to stop the thoughts and my body from visibly shaking.

He asked me if I had anything to say, as these would be my last words before I died. I said, "Tell my children that I love them." This infuriated him and he fired the shot. I winced and closed my eyes, instinctively raising my arms to my chest. The noise was deafening. The bullet missed its target, hitting the metal weight bench just behind me instead. I opened my eyes to see him reloading the second cartridge. Panicking, I quickly looked around for something to defend myself with, but there was nothing. Shall I tackle him? Were the kids awake? Were they going to come into the bedroom wondering what that noise was? Or were they lying in bed, terrified and huddled together, with their little hands over their ears? My heart was pounding so hard I couldn't think properly. I couldn't run and I couldn't fight. Someone heard that shot? Please, this time, someone call the police. I knew the shot had been heard but knew nobody would get involved. His reputation for violence preceded him; they were rightfully fearful of the consequences. They all knew, they saw me with black eyes, cuts and bruises, but nobody ever asked me if I was ok. They just avoided me until they were no longer visible.

Moments later the loaded gun was again aimed at my stomach and the pressure of fear creeping up my spine kept rising, and I couldn't breathe in properly. I watched, in slow motion, as his finger slowly pulled the trigger towards him. It wasn't the fear of dying I felt; I didn't want my children to come into the room and see me in that state. I didn't want the mental images of me framed and hung up like a prize possession in the gallery of their minds. I didn't want them to know the smell of fear before death. I didn't want them to remember the sounds of that night, triggering unwanted memories in their future. I didn't want them to experience the bitterness, the sour taste of hate and regret, and I didn't want the energy of this to touch their hearts so they could no longer feel the love inside them. I wanted more for them, they deserved so much more...

Everything slowed down. I recall hearing a bird outside the window. At first, it was a slight sound, but very quickly gained momentum, getting louder and louder. It was singing its little heart out. It was so gentle and so clear, as if trying to convince me to focus on it and, as I listened intently, I became so completely engulfed in the moment. In my mind I said, 'It's ok; God will look after it all. My children are God's children; they will be loved and cared for. I know this," and I let go of all thought. As I did so, a rush of calm, a sweet surrender, a feeling of peace and pure love came over me. A feeling of complete nothingness, but at the same time everything, completely enveloped me. It was inside me and surrounding me in this beautiful place of no thought. All I could hear was the bird. It wasn't that I no longer cared; I just had no thoughts to care... mind, body and soul were free.

I was unaware of time and don't know how long I was surrounded by love, but eventually, the bird stopped singing and I came back to the present moment. The gun had been triggered but the cartridge had bent in the barrel, preventing it from firing. He told me I was lucky, and I just looked at him. He was suddenly overcome with tiredness and was now fearful of me. Fearful thoughts of what I might do while he slept rose up in him, but they were all of his own making, they were his thoughts and didn't belong to me. He told me to lie on the bed next to him and I did. I lay there with the gun between us, replaying, over and over, the movie that I had just starred in. My home, growing up, had been the one place I felt safe, but now my home had become the one place to fear, making my outer world seem so much more peaceful. I thought of the day ahead and how I would get up and go about my day. How I would see and greet people, and nobody would know that today would have been a different day had that cartridge not bent. I closed my eyes, breathing in deeply, remembering and feeling into the beautiful place I had just been taken too. The feeling would never totally leave me again. I would flit in and out of it consciously, but it would never leave me, as I now knew where and what home really was and I no longer feared death, anything or anyone.

Free from Fear reflections

When you hide from your pain or try to use tools to dull it, it doesn't go away for long, and for some people these tools allow it to escape. It becomes dysfunctional and destructive, infecting everyone around it. He was never aware in these moments; he was completely missing and that was where the danger lay.

Pain is not something you can subdue or pretend isn't there, as it will creep up on you. It's only when you no longer try to hide the pain and face it head on, seeing it for what it is, contrast showing you which way to go, how to be, or not to be, that you will use it for what it gave you. When you master this, the pain transforms into wisdom.

*This person he was when he drank was not who he really was. I knew his spirit was calling him, but he couldn't hear it through his anger. His soul was turning over and over in his body, trying to get his attention, but he couldn't feel it through numbing himself. When I met him, I saw such potential in him. He was extremely alive, clever, strong and funny, and the possibilities for him to evolve into a great example of a man was evident, but he allowed the pain inside him to overtake his potential, batting away his opportunities and crippling possibilities. Instead of finding himself, he hid himself in a cocktail of destructive substances and, instead of allowing his spirit to lead the way, he allowed the spirit of the bottle to take him over.

When you are in a situation like the one I found myself in, your mind works overtime. Different scenarios come up and thoughts fuelled in fear surface and take such a hold of you, so you cannot think or feel clearly. A great imagination is a wonderful thing to have and is very powerful at creating, but it can also add more fuel to any situation you find yourself in.

I learnt a superpower by being in these situations, going deeper within to find control over my mind and body. Breathing is underrated and, just because we breathe in and out every second, it doesn't mean we are breathing correctly. Learning how to breathe was a lifesaver for me, in more ways than one.

I didn't blame people for not getting involved, but it did make me feel like nobody cared. I hid it from my parents and siblings as I knew they couldn't do anything, so why share the burden?

It's funny how, once the cartridge bent, it was suddenly all over. He suddenly came over, all tired, and then he became fearful of me. I was still full of light and felt nothing; he could feel the energy, the power and was fearful of going to sleep. There was nothing to fear but the fearful thoughts going around in his own head. In that moment I realised he was not powerful at all, just full of fear.

There is great freedom in gaining control of your own vibration, even when the vibration of fear surrounds you.

In that sweet state of surrender anything could happen, and it did. Once I had surrendered, feeling the energy, the light engulfing me, I was no longer a match for the damage the cartridge would do to my body.

Living this way took its toll on me, and made me feel like I was dying inside, but this experience showed me I was not ready to die yet and there was a bigger purpose for my life, and I began to live again. There was nothing to fear but fear itself.

I knew this didn't mean I'd never feel fear again. It meant I could learn to become the master of it. I knew that Earth was not my home, I was just a visitor on a mission, and I had nothing to fear because I was a child of God.

It's the gaps between the notes that make the music. It's the space between the letters that make the word. In the stillness of your mind is where you hear the whisper of your soul. It's that place of 'no thing' where everything is found.

All thought is food

Food for thought, or, all thought is food. We are feeding ourselves constantly, moment by moment, with our thoughts. Every image, everything we see, taste, touch, hear and smell, leaves a memory, an imprint, either negatively or positively, and they are all stored in our mind. We can't always help what goes in, but we are responsible for what we choose to keep and focus on. Once you know how powerful your thoughts are, and how they are the very beginning of whatever you are creating, you become selective, choosing wisely, because you know the impact it will have on your life. Even so, creating just with the mind has its limitations. It is when you silence the mind that you tap into the bigger part of you, where every received thought comes straight from a place of consciousness, where the realms of possibilities for creating are limitless.

Perception of God. What does the word God mean to you? For me, God is not a man up in the sky that watches over us all, dishing out blessings and punishments. God is Love, and when I say love, this will also bring up thoughts and feelings as to your perception of love and what it means to you personally. The love I speak about is not the anaemic, watered down version of love most of us encounter. The love of God is pure, undiluted; it's a flow of never-ending joy. It is always flowing to you in its pureness and sees you only in your true essence and nothing less. Focusing only on your divine heart of love and allowing your own free will to bring you the experiences that will assist you in remembering, that as you were created from this love, you are nothing less than this love.

In the beginning there was you. You bravely came to Earth to fulfil your mission and were born into environments that would allow the seeds of greatness to take root. You were fully aligned with source, and the crown at the top of your head was soft and open allowing the pure energy of light to flow easily to and through you. Before the conditioning began you were fearless, limitless and full of wonder, and your heartbeat with the rhythm of love, but it wasn't long before the soft spot began to harden, as you were taught by those around you how to think, act and how to feel. You thought you had no choice but to listen, as those with the loudest voices spoke their truth and felt the disempowerment as your limited beliefs restricted the seeds of greatness inside you. You wanted to be happy and free, but were spoon-fed fear. This felt unnatural to you, making you feel disconnected, as love is your natural frequency. You slowly conformed to beliefs that did not belong to you and had no place in your mind. You allowed the pain of your experiences to lead the way, thinking this was punishment for an unworthy soul such as yours, but that isn't so my warriors. Free will is your birthright; you can choose the way you live. Your creator is not punishing you, life is responding to you and the vibration you give out. You can either choose to stay in the negative experiences you encountered, allowing the pain to replay over and over, and emitting a vibration out into the world, attracting more of the same to you, reaffirming the vibration, or you can do what you came to do, learn the valuable lessons it offered, push through the pain and unfold and emerge into the true light being you are.

Death is not the end. We are energy in a body. When our body dies, we escape the confines of our mind and vibrate in the frequency of love again. We can still communicate with our loved ones, sometimes better than when they were in physical form, as they are no longer holding onto emotions, they are free. They feel no regret and there is nothing to forgive, as they are unconditional love once more. It is natural to feel pain as a loved one departs from this dimension, but as you elevate your vibration to one of love, you are vibrating on the same frequency and are a match to hear, see and feel them, and you can ask them to be an angel of light, assisting you from their higher vantage point.

Meditation is the key to unlocking the secrets of the universe. When we connect directly with Source and stop the chatter of our mind, we align with thoughts and feelings of a higher nature. We can feel the limitless potential and the emerging of our true essence and sit comfortably in the chair of Knowledge, knowing that anything is possible. There is no need to look to others to lead you or show you the way to the truth, because in connecting directly with Source, you will feel the truth. As this connection grows, we no longer care what others think of us, as we know they are on their own journey and what they think is just their perception. We see behaviour as the playing out of what is going on internally, taking nothing personally and seeing others in their true light. This is very freeing and assists the seeds inside us to find a way to the surface.

I choose to connect directly to Source and be guided by my own inner light, instead of following any particular religion. I see truth in all of them, to some degree, and I have no judgement as to what is wrong or right for anyone else, but it should be a choice, as we have to follow our own path.

The power is in focusing, not on the issues, but on the solutions. You have to start believing you are a powerful being, and the bigger part of you is energy. You are not your mind or your body, you are conscious energy. I believe the best way of releasing negative emotions that are not serving your highest good is to stop talking about what occurred. No longer going over the details of it, trying to make sense of it all, but rather to look for the lesson it taught, the superpowers it gave you and the pressure it put your seeds of greatness under so they could become diamonds to be released out of you. Every time you talk about something, you feed it, you bring it to life with your thoughts and, when you speak, you release from your throat the sounds and vibrations of those thoughts, speaking into existence the very sounds you vibrate out. You have to become conscious in every moment with what you are creating. You cannot change the past, it's done. All your power is in the Now, and that you do have control over. Start creating the life you deserve and one you are more than worthy of.

◊ ◊ ◊ ◊

We have seven primary energy centres in our body. Each centre is like a sphere, a spinning ball of pure energy. They sit along your spine at different locations, each one looking after the relevant parts assigned to them and, as they spin, they radiate energy out into your body. This energy can be seen clearly in young children who have not yet had their spheres clogged up by the negative imprints of their minds.

It's easy to see how thought affects all these energy centres and how they get clogged up with negative imprints of thought turning to feelings, slowing them down so they are not vibrating properly and sending out the energy needed by your body to maintain its health and vitality. If your centre remains in this state for any length of time, it causes discomfort and dis-ease.

First – Red – When we stop letting our thoughts of insecurity get the better of us, no matter what circumstances we were born into, and replace them with the knowledge that we are here for a reason, we are here on purpose and it's time to open ourselves up to our mission, we claim and affirm… "I live for a reason. I live because I have purpose. I live as an example of the light that is within me."

Second - Orange - When we stop holding onto the shame of any unconscious behaviour and begin to feel what each experience has to teach us. If something you said or did, made you feel good, then do more, but if it didn't, you know it's not for you, so move on, releasing the emotion, as it no longer serves you. We start to affirm… "I feel joyful. I feel creative energy flowing. I feel like a river, always moving, forever changing and evolving."

Third - Yellow - When we realise free will is our birthright and use the free will given to us from Source, not just for our own good, but for the good of all, we are no longer lead by others, but instead, choose to be the example for others. We feel our own light and power and begin to affirm… "I do what I want to do. I do things the bigger part of me nudges me to do. I do when it is time to do."

Fourth - Green - When we open our hearts and allow the protective layers to peel away, we remember that unconditional love is our natural state and anything less than this for ourselves and for others is not enough. We can affirm… "I love myself completely and unconditionally. I love others as I love myself. I love because this is my natural frequency."

Fifth - Blue - When we express our truth honestly and calmly we allow the flow of energy to be felt through our words. There is no longer a need to lie, as there is no need to hide, and we share our truth openly and honestly and allow others the same right, as it no longer matters whether your truth matches the views of others. You firmly and proudly affirm… "I speak my truth. I speak clearly, openly and honestly. I speak with consciousness."

Sixth - Indigo - When we no longer view the world with two eyes but look through with the vision of the third, we see our world is ours for the creating. Our world turns from opaque to crystal clear and we 'real-eyes' we have been living in a world of illusion. With clear vision and a new view on life we move into co-creating the world we always dreamed of living in. We affirm… "I see at last. I see the world from my open eye. I see things as I am creating them to be."

Seventh - Violet - When we connect directly with the source of all life and open the crown of our head to let in the flow of light energy that is always focused and flowing to us, we begin to understand it was never taken away and we were never disconnected, it was our own thoughts that stopped the flow. We felt this disconnection of the life force energy deep within us and tried to fill the gaping hole with things and people, but nothing compares and so, at last, we affirm… "I am real love and I know where I come from. I am a unique spark of the divine. I am not here to live by others' interpretation of what is life, but to create my own."

We have a rainbow of colours inside us that are there to spin and dance in vibrational harmony. When we stop blaming others and take responsibility for ourselves, we see we have the healing power to dissolve the emotions we have held on to so tightly, and allow the lesson in each experience to be understood on a deeper level. We finally release our energy centres from the bondage we created, allowing them to spin in harmony with each other, sending out vitality, light and energy to every cell of our bodies. As we move out of this dimension and into the higher states of consciousness, the colours of our energy centres will change to integrate the new light within us, and we will become, once again, the true light being we always were.

I know you have felt the pull of spirit and asked many times what is the purpose of it all, as you saw people hurting each other, witnessed injustice and felt pain. You have desired a better world, one built on compassion and love, where understanding and nurturing is at the forefront, but it starts with you. Once you have mastered yourself, gaining control over your thoughts and releasing old emotions, you will see how, individually, you play a powerful part in changing 'what is' to what we want it to be.

We get so distracted and caught up in 'what is' that we are not tapping into our true abilities. We did not come to accept things as they are, but to create a better way to be. As each of us focuses internally, clearing the mind and body from beliefs that no longer serve us, we attract like-minded, like-hearted beings to us. As we come together as a collective consciousness, not just for our own good but for the good of all, our individual soul song rings out in perfect harmony with each other's, in a powerful unified version of sound, and in tune with the frequency of love.

Printed in Great Britain
by Amazon

78469438R00113